A Call to Covenant Relationship

George Peart

ISBN: 1-59684-107-9

©Copyright 2005 by George W. Peart
All Rights Reserved
Printed by Derek Press, Cleveland, TN

Acknowledgement

The content of this book is a series of sermons inspired by the Holy Spirit for the benefit of the believers. Although the idea of covenant is not a new idea, the approach and presentation is.

All of us who attempt to put ideas in writing know that it takes the efforts of dedicated friends and associates.

Two such persons that I'm deeply indebted to for reading and corrections are Dr. T.L. Grizzle and Dr. Leonard Lovett. Others who have encouraged me to put the ideas in book form are:

Reverend Walter Francis, Reverend Marcella Lewis, Reverend Courtney Williams, just to name a few.

Dedication

This book is dedicated to the West Toronto Church of God for their inspiration and encouragement and to Jireta my wife for allowing me time to be able to complete this book.

Preface

The author, George Peart, takes readers on a Biblical journey that will enhance and strengthen their lives. He establishes the fact that God is a covenant-making and a covenant-keeping God. In the very beginning of time, in the Garden of Eden, He began to fashion a relationship with mankind. The Bible emphasizes that the very heartbeat of the Creator is to have communion and fellowship with His creation. Furthermore, we are brought to the realization that mankind is created with the resources to have such fellowship and communion.

The author points out that the primary reason for so much unhappiness in the world today is that mankind has broken that fellowship with God. The very reason Christ lived and died was for us to have that personal relationship with God. Until we begin to walk in that divine covenant relationship, we will never find complete fulfillment and happiness in our lives.

Not only does the author emphasize this covenant relationship between God and man, he also brings us to the fact that the same Biblical principles should be followed in the relationship between man and wife. If these Biblical principles are applied in the home, then the marriage relationship can be strengthened. Also, if believers apply these principles to the church and its ministry, then the Kingdom of God will increase and their lives will be blessed.

This is a great book for personal Bible study, church Bible study, cell groups and marriage seminars.

Jerry Puckett
Director, Derek Press

Contents

A Call to Covenant 1

Difference Between Covenant and Promise 21

Covenant – A Binding Relationship 31

After the Honeymoon. 41

Family and Worship 59

Covenant Bonding of the Natural and Spiritual 67

Introduction

Dr. George Peart has been a pastor for nearly forty years, the broad sweep of his pastoral ministry encompassing churches in England, Canada, and the USA. My dear and trusted friend for as many years, he has been an uncluttered megaphone for truth, an undimmed beacon of integrity, and a model of true servant leadership over the years. The contents of this book on covenant relationship reflect the practical insights and distilled wisdom of one who knows how to pitch the Word of God at the wavelength of human need and inspire God's people to a higher life of conformity to the image of Christ.

A common and necessary part of both religious and secular life in the ancient world, covenant making which governed relationships among countries, people, and the worship of deity is nearly as old as the human race. While the concept has little or no prevailing influence on human relations in the modern world, covenant still regulates the way God relates to His people today. God is a God of covenant.

In *Covenant Relationships*, Dr. Peart explores the concept of covenant and shows that covenant and contract are neither identical nor interchangeable. Biblically defined,

A Call to Covenant Relationship

a covenant is a sovereign dispensing of grace followed by benefits and obligations. A contract or a bilateral agreement has an end date. God's covenant is permanent and carries serious consequences if violated—a fact intimated in the Hebrew root word, which means "to cut a covenant." The notion of cutting a covenant points to the custom of the two covenanting parties sealing an agreement by passing through the split body of a slain animal (Jer.34:8), invoking upon themselves the same fate as befell the animal should they violate the covenant.

The permanent and binding nature of covenant means that none of God's covenants are ever truly displaced by later ones; they are merely enriched, enhanced, and bring God's grace to a higher level of expression. Viewing God's covenant relationship with His people in marital and familial terms, Dr. Peart artfully depicts God as a suitor who, beginning in the Garden of Eden, woos his beloved, marries her and ultimately settles down with her in the beautiful home he prepared for her (Rev. 21:1-4). Throughout the Old and New Testaments covenant governed and guided God's actions towards His people. Today He still reaches out to His children through covenant love, and His people can expect Him to act on their behalf because of His irrevocable covenant commitment to us.

> Dr. Trevor Grizzle
> Professor of New Testament
> Oral Roberts University

A Call to Covenant Relationship

Part I

But *I will establish my covenant with you; and you shall go into the ark—you, your sons, your wife, and your sons' wives with you.'"* (Gen. 6:18, NKJV)

Covenant making is nearly as old as the human race. It was a common and necessary part of religious and secular life in the ancient world, governing relationships among countries, people, and the worship of deity.

What is a "covenant"? Webster defines it as a mutual and solemn agreement, a contract or a compact. A covenant is a solemn promise made binding by an oath. From a Biblical perspective, the most frequent word used to designate it is the Hebrew *berit*. Occurring 286 times in the Old Testament, it refers to a **"league or confederacy,"** and is most likely derived from an Akkadian root meaning to **"fetter."** It has parallels in Hittite, Egyptian, Assyrian and Aramaic. Its Greek equivalent **(diatheke)** often carries the idea of **"last will and testament."**

A Call to Covenant Relationship

While there were many types of covenants and various conditions and degrees of penalties to which the covenanting parties were bound, covenants generally fell under three main categories in the ancient world: *royal grant, suzerain-vassal,* and *parity.*

The royal grant was a king's gift to a loyal servant for faithful or exceptional service. It was normally unconditional and perpetual, and benefited the servant's heirs if they remained faithful to the king. In a suzerain-vassal covenant, a great king claimed absolute sovereignty over a subject king, demanding total loyalty and pledging to him protection for faithfulness. A parity covenant was made between equals, binding them to mutual friendship or respect.

Agreements made in these covenants were accompanied by self-maledictory oaths, and the presence of the gods invoked to witness the covenants and implement the curses should they be violated. The Old Testament records seven major covenants between God and his people, five royal grants and two suzerain-vassals. Understandably, no parity covenant exists since no human person can claim equality with God. Noah was the first participant in a royal-grant covenant (Gen. 9:8-17), followed by Abraham who participated in both a royal-grant (Gen. 15:9-21) and a suzerain-vassal covenant (Gen. 17). Exodus 19-24 records the suzerain-vassal covenant between God and Israel.

Both the zealous priest, Phinehas (Num. 25:10-13) and King David (2 Sam. 7:5-16) were parties to royal-grant covenants. God's promise to unfaithful Israel through Jeremiah (31:31-34) to forgive her sins and establish a new relationship with her based upon writing his law "on their hearts" constituted the final royal-grant covenant—a covenant of grace.

Part I

In the Biblical sense, a covenant is far weightier than a contract or a simple agreement, and reveals the strength and permanence of God's relationship with his people. Whereas a contract has an end date, a covenant is permanent and carries serious consequences if violated. Such terrible consequences are intimated in the Hebrew root word, which means "to cut a covenant." The word points to the custom of the two covenanting parties sealing an agreement by passing through the split body of a slain animal (Jer. 34:8), invoking upon themselves the same fate as befell the animal should they violate the covenant.

For the lack of a better backdrop, I want to set this study of covenant in the context of marriage and the family, because in modern society, it is the context to which most people can relate and, indeed, one in which the very essence of covenant is played out. Furthermore, more than any other covenant, marriage represents the depth of the divine-human relationship, the permanence of that bond, and the blessings that flow from it.

Before we get to the covenant of marriage, it is important to examine briefly a preliminary process that is customary in probably all societies: "mate selection." It may be said that while marriage is technically the beginning phase of family life, mate selection is a necessary precursor to marriage.

Family life comprises the process of two persons joining together, resulting usually in the reproduction of children, nurturing, and eventually separating from them. Mate selection is that point at which two individuals decide to separate from their parents and unite to form their own family or a new living relationship. This takes place before the two people move to covenanting in marriage. Understanding

A Call to Covenant Relationship

mate selection, then, is important for understanding the other stages in the life cycle of the family.

The reason I choose initially to couch this study in the context of the family is that the first six chapters of Genesis can be seen as an allegory in which God seeks to establish a family. Although the term "covenant" in scripture first appears in Genesis 6:18 (*"Behold I will establish my covenant with you [Noah]"*), the idea occurs earlier in that book where I see someone who is engaged to be married but through deception gets into a relationship with a jealous suitor. Indeed, it seems to me that God was in love with Adam and Eve, but another man sneaked in and told them not to trust everything that God said, thus destroying the courtship.

Take one step backwards. Look at God in his creative acts in Genesis 1 and 2. Allow your imagination to run wild. Does God not look like a good man preparing a pleasing and complete environment in which He hopes to spend a lifetime with His soul mate? I am aware that the imagery or form of speech I employ is anthropomorphic, but that's okay. It's been employed over and over in scripture. In the Prophets, Israel is referred to many times as the wife of Jehovah.

In Genesis 1:1, the writer gives a brief glimpse of an eternity not known to us: *"In the beginning God created the heavens and the earth."* In verse 2 we are told, *"the earth was without form, and void; and that darkness was on the face of the deep."* You don't have to be a rocket scientist or even a theologian to know that everything that God ever created is perfect. We may infer, therefore, that a lost world existed between verse one and verse two. We also know that the latter part of the verse—*"and the Spirit of God was*

Part I

hovering over the face of the waters" refers to a creative process which brought our present creation into existence, because God said immediately thereafter, *"Let there be light, and there was light."*

This light that suddenly sprang out of the darkness is the creative act of God in Christ, for John says of Jesus, *"In the beginning was the Word, and the Word was with God, and the Word was God. ... All things were made through Him. ... In Him was life, and the life was the light of men"* (John 1:1, 3, 4; see also Col. 1:16). Like a caring spouse, in this creative act God brought about beauty by bringing light into the world. Jesus is the light of the world. He is the light that makes all things possible. In the beginning, He shone not only to separate the light from the darkness, thereby, making possible a habitable world; He shone also in the heart of sinful man, thereby making his heart habitable by the Spirit of God. It is this twofold work that uniquely marks and initiates God's search for a special relationship with the crown of His creation—man.

God did first things first, for without light, nothing proceeds. If only we could put first things first for God! What a difference it would make!

Once God had given us light, note the next thing He did. He called for a "firmament" above (v. 6). In olden days, in preparation for marriage, a man would build a booth or a canopy to shelter the bride and her bridal party from the elements. Should it rain on the wedding day, the bride and her party would be sheltered. Neither rain nor sun would hinder the wedding.

So did God, when He separated the waters above from the waters beneath. He prepared a canopy for man, the one with whom He would develop a covenant relationship, the

A Call to Covenant Relationship

one with whom He would walk throughout the ages.

Once the canopy was built, something for the feet, something to add beauty and aesthetic grandeur was necessary. So God said, *"Let the earth bring forth grass, the herb that yields seed"* (v. 11). Then He called for the light in the firmament—the canopy. Who can carry out a wedding party without light, especially in cultures where a wedding-party could go on for days or even weeks?

The land being arid, God made the necessary food sources by which the human family could be nurtured and sustained. Preparation for a covenant relationship is expanding and intensifying, more clearly evident in Genesis 2:8: *"Then the Lord God planted a garden eastward in Eden; and there he put the man whom he had formed."* Having put everything into their hands, He blessed them and enjoined them to *"be fruitful and multiply; fill the earth and subdue it"* (1:28).

Alas, in chapter 3 we come face to face with another man (the serpent) that discredited the first intended spouse. Being relentless, he succeeded in turning the mind of man from God his creator. Yet, this deceptive act of the serpent served only to bring out more clearly the love relationship between God and the crown of His creation—man, because 3: 8-9 says that Adam and Eve *"heard the sound of the Lord walking in the garden in the cool of the day: and Adam and his wife hid themselves from the presence of the Lord God among the trees of the garden. Then the Lord called to Adam and said to him, 'where are you?'"* Lovers always look for companionship with the one they love.

It is significant that though God's creation was vast, God specifically placed the love of His heart and the apple of His eye in an exclusive and specifically prepared place—the garden. Who can deny that this has the face of one trying to build a love relationship? Tragically, all this was to be thwarted by the deceptive devices of Satan. The rest of Genesis 3 evidences the indictment of the man and his ultimate expulsion from the garden and the presence of God—just like a failed courtship!

In Genesis 4, we encounter the next person with whom God wished to establish a love relationship—Abel. Sadly, Abel was killed by his own brother, Cain, and by the end of the chapter we discover two murders and a lifestyle of multiple wives. That's evidence enough that sin was becoming rampant upon the face of the earth. It also tells us that the longer man lived, both proverbially and literally, the more wicked he became.

Chapter 6 is undeniable proof that man had become so corrupt and defiant that the **sons of God** saw **the daughters of men** and began to admire them. **Sons of God** refer to the lineage of Seth, the chosen ones by which God intended to restore the covenant relationship. **The daughters of men** are the descendants of Cain, children of a murderer. May I suggest to you that the term *to admire* does not merely imply to look at.

To admire something or someone is to be fascinated by that thing or that someone. And the idea of being fascinated suggests the capturing of one's mind and attention, and the mind and attention cannot be totally separated from the soul. Therefore, if you admire or are fascinated by something or by someone, and fail to take radical steps to correct it, before long your mind will be completely taken over by the object of its attraction.

That was the kind of admiration that the sons of God had for the daughters of men. They were enthralled by them, which would in the final analysis create an unholy alliance

A Call to Covenant Relationship

that would interfere with the whole plan of redemption. For He that would redeem us must be of a pure lineage. He that cleanses must first be clean. Little did Seth's descendants know that their temptation came from the same devil that deceived Adam and Eve earlier in the garden. Satan merely changed his clothes, not his destructive intention. He was back with a new bag of tricks aimed at thwarting the plan of God that was intended to bring about the salvation of man.

If Satan can't take you out one way, he will try another, and another. If persistence were his middle name, it would be most appropriate. If you missed him for a while, do not let down your guard; he's merely working out a new plan and new logistics. Just you wait, he'll be back—and often with a vengeance.

Nothing angers God faster than when the church and the world begin to cohabit. For out of such cohabitation can only come monsters—"fallen ones," as the Hebrew word *nephilim* connotes in chapter 6:4. Tragically, **the fallen ones** became the heroes of the people. Yet, nothing that God has to do with can turn out entirely wrong, for many of **"the fallen ones"** became men of renown. After all, the blood of Seth, God's chosen vessel, ran through their veins; Cain's descendants partook of the blessings of Seth by association. And so, even though **"the fallen ones"** came out of a union not approved by God, God could not entirely disenfranchise them.

Several hundred years are compressed in Genesis 1-6. They contain the lives of numerous people, including Adam, who lived 930 years, Cain, Abel, Seth, and Methuselah the longest liver of all—969 years. Yet, not until Enoch was it said that anyone *"walked with God"* (5:24). Before Enoch,

Part I

men merely lived. Enoch walked with God. There is a big difference between merely living and walking with God. Of course, God took Enoch away.

God had always been looking for someone who would walk with Him. For two cannot walk unless they be agreed! In order to make a covenant, God must find a man with whom He could walk. Walking together is suggestive of communication, and God can communicate only with a person who walks in righteousness before Him. This is "**divine romance.**"

Note carefully that Methuselah was the son of Enoch, the man who walked with God, the man that God took. Methuselah lived the longest of all human beings as we know it—969 years. It is apparent that walking with God pays off, not only for the one who walks with Him, but also for his progeny. But better yet, Enoch himself who walked with God did not die. God took him. As early as Genesis 5 God began to give evidence to man that walking with Him has unusual benefits in this life and the life to come.

Anyone who has been saved for any length of time knows that walking with God cannot be likened to a cute little puppy-dog following its master wagging its tail. Any person who dares to walk with God, be it in this age, in ages past, or in ages to come, must suffer persecution and endure denial of self. But such persons are promised life everlasting, *"for they that suffer with Him shall also reign with him."*

Given the tempo of things by this time, Enoch, having chosen to walk with God, must have been a man of sturdy character. He must have endured his fair share of persecution and ridicule. Little wonder God rewarded him with escaping the one thing that man dreads most—death.

A Call to Covenant Relationship

God will give his followers life eternal as he did Enoch, but **their progeny shall also be blessed.** For Enoch had Methuselah and Methuselah had Lamech and Lamech had Noah. The man who was found trustworthy enough by God so that He could tell him the secret of His heart in respect to the future, unbelievable though it seemed, obeyed to the glory of God and the saving of his family, and ultimately of the world. Men that will dare to walk with God will always be blessed, but there will also always be a blessing to their family and to their generation.

After great persistence and unfailing patience, God found a man that he could covenant with. To this man he declared, *"But I will establish my covenant with you"* (6:18). But note the preamble to establishing the covenant: *"So the Lord said, 'I will destroy man whom I have created from the face of the earth... '"* (v. 7) *"But Noah found grace [unmerited favor] in the eyes of the Lord"* (v. 8) *"This is the genealogy of Noah. Noah was a just man, perfect in his generations. Noah walked with God"* (v. 9).

It is this kind of person and this kind of interaction God seeks in order to form a permanent relationship, a relationship that looks like **"mate selection and marriage."** A man of grace, a just man, a man of perfection—the right ingredients for a relationship that is intimate! **"I will establish my contract, my pact, my alliance, my covenant with you,"** God said to Noah. **Why a Covenant?**

We should observe in the first place that a covenant and a promise are not the same. We earlier defined covenant. So, let us now define promise. Webster defines promise as *"an undertaking to do, or not to do something - a cause or grounds for hope, to give cause or hope for expectation, to agree to give, to assure by a promise."* A promise can

Part I

be broken, but a covenant cannot; and if it is broken, it has consequences far beyond those of a promise.

You and I are all too acquainted with broken hearts which, if heaped up along the highway of life, would rival the pyramids of Egypt. We know of broken promises which would stop the heart of a rhinoceros. Some people were promised marriage, but got pregnant instead. Some were promised love, but got hate instead. Some were promised protection; abuse was their lot instead. A home, even a penthouse, was the attractive reward pledged by a dashing suitor; a life of hell in a shack was the reality.

Some people have experienced so many broken promises that they have difficulty trusting, even trusting God. They have taken literally the old cliche, *"Once bitten twice shy."* Or should I say, once bitten *"forever shy."* Many have even swallowed hook line and sinker the adage that *"promise is a comfort to a fool."* And who can blame them? No one needs to experience a broken heart but once.

This is why so-called uncivilized man, discovering that promises could be, and were often, broken devised his own way of ensuring that promises made to him were kept. It was required that two covenanting men cut their hands and place both bleeding hands together so that the blood from each would be absorbed by the other. Hence, when they parted, the two people had the same blood running in their veins. The two people were now truly one.

Truly one, uniquely one! Such was the relationship between Jesus and his Father. Jesus said, *"I and the Father are one"* (Jn. 10:30). Again, He declared, *"Anyone who has seen me has seen the Father. ... Don't you believe that I am in the Father, and that the Father is in me?"* (Jn. 14:9-10). It was this relationship that inspired the words, *"My food is*

A Call to Covenant Relationship

to do the will of Him who sent me and to finish His work" (Jn. 4:34).

This is the kind of relationship that God seeks with His people. His blood runs through our veins. We are His. We are one with Christ. That is why the promise without a "permanent contract" (covenant) will not do. A covenant locks in and puts a long-term demand upon the relationship, pretty much like a lady saying to a suitor, *"No wed, no bed. No contract, no contact. No ring, no ding."*

Another shortcoming of a promise, as opposed to a contract, is that more often than not a promise is extended only to the person or persons to whom the promise is made. A covenant, however, is usually extended even to the progeny for generations to come. Note the story as told in Genesis 6:18. *"But I will establish my covenant with you; and you will enter the ark-you and your sons, and your wife, and your sons' wives with you."* Genesis 9:1 says, *"Then God blessed Noah and his sons,"* and in verses 8-10, *"Then God said to Noah and to his sons with him: 'I now establish my covenant with you and with your descendants after you and with every living creature that was with you. . . . "* I say again, there is a world of difference between a promise and a covenant.

Just in case you forgot the whole idea of mate selection, which I mentioned earlier, let me say here again that many thousands of years had elapsed by now, and God, as it were, has finally found someone with whom He can walk. Someone with whom He can talk. One who will obey His will. One who will cooperate with His program. Noah represents the hope and new direction for the future for all of human life; in him God will give humankind a second chance at life upon the earth.

Part I

The awesome power of one! Upon one obedient man rests the future and destiny of the earth. One person makes a difference. We should never underestimate the influence and potential of a single life lived in obedience to God. Let us not follow the crowd. One person and God can be the majority.

God's invitation to Noah and his family earlier in 7:1 is pregnant with meaning. Let's turn there for a moment. *"Then the Lord said to Noah, 'Come into the ark, you and all your household, because I have seen that you are righteous before Me in this generation'" (NKJV).* Wow! Isn't God uniting the relationship, just like a lover in search of a spouse.

If you have an eye for words, take a close look at this one: **"COME .... You and all your household."** **"Come"** is an abbreviation of **"Come here."** No one can call you to a place he is not. Come intimates that the Ark is God's idea of protecting His family in the flood. **"Come"** suggests that God was in the Ark. **"Come"** instructs that the Ark is His. **"Come"** informs that He will be there with them throughout the days of the flood. Not only Noah, but all that is with him. Because, you see, the blessing will come, not only to him but anything that is with him. **This is divine romance.**

Noah, having obeyed the voice of the Lord, made the Ark. When the work was completed, God commanded him to embark and lock the door to make sure that no one talked him into opening it once the rains began to fall.

There is a time for calling upon God. It is today, if you hear His voice. Not when the rain of God's wrath begins to fall. Not when the door is locked. Notice that there is but one door. There is but one way to come to God: by faith. You must be able to believe while the Ark is still being built—

A Call to Covenant Relationship

before you understand it *all!*—*"because anyone that comes to him, must believe that he exists and that he rewards those who earnestly seek him"* (Heb. 11:6).

There is a dispensation of grace, at which time all you have to do is look to Jesus and live. But when God's time is full, when the door is locked, it is too late. The fact that God himself locked the Ark not only prevented anyone from talking Noah into letting others in, but also suggests that God kept the keys. And the keeper of the keys is the final authority! He alone decides who goes in and who comes out.

The authority that keys represent is both preventative and protective. As sovereign Lord with final authority (Rev. 1:8), Jesus told John, *"hold the keys of death and of Hades"* (Rev. 1: 18). You may go through Jesus, but not around Him, or under Him, or above Him. You must come in at the door. He is the door, and He alone has the keys.

Of course, as you might well know, by informing the apostle John that He holds the key, Jesus is also informing John that his life is in the hand of none other than His. Life and death are in the hands of the keeper of the keys. Be he on the Isle of Patmos or any other place, the apostle cannot be harmed, for Christ alone holds the keys.

There is more to learn from the life of Noah. He and his family and all the animals once safely in the Ark, it began to rain—the first time it had rained since the creation of the earth (see Gen. 2:6). It was a hundred and fifty days later before we hear anything from him (Gen. 7:24). The flood waters now receded, he sent out a raven to test the water level. The raven did not return. Then he sent out a dove, which returned without resting, indicating that the waters had not receded sufficiently for Noah to disembark from the ark. Seven days later, he sent out a dove again. This time it brought back an olive branch of hope, signaling that it was safe to vacate the Ark on Mount Ararat (8:7-12), perhaps the only safe place for the soles of their feet.

What follows must not by any means be taken lightly. The implications are indeed instructive: *"Then Noah built an altar unto the Lord and, taking some of all the clean animals and clean birds, he sacrificed burnt offerings on it"* (8:20). Noah's first look after realizing God's great deliverance was Godward—upward, not outward. His first act was to erect an altar, not build a home. The spiritual took primacy over the physical.

Noah started over with God. What ordering of priorities! Starting life with God and starting life with worship.

If I understood this story right, the animals that Noah took into the ark were not for consumption, but for breeding. They were to replenish the earth, just as Noah and his family were to replenish the earth with people. Despite the limited livestock he had, to Noah nothing was too good for God. Nothing was so restricted so as to withhold from God a part. And notice that he gave of the clean animal, the best! That's the nature of covenant. Once you are in a covenant relationship with God, nothing is too good for you to give to Him.

Covenant giving realizes that everything we have belongs to God in the first place. Not giving to God is a sure sign that one is not in a covenant relationship with Him. Besides, it shows a lack of understanding of the economy of God, i.e., to give is to get. To give your best, is to get His best. That is, giving to God represents multiplication rather than subtraction.

I am profoundly moved by this act of faith and trust on the part of Noah. This man represents faith and obedience at their best. The average human would first think of the value of those animals, their costliness in light of their scarcity. Breeding would probably be a foremost concern. But such is not the nature of covenant relationship. In covenant relationship, all that are ours are his also. The very best we have belongs to Him.

Noah has offered his sacrifice to God. Now comes the divine response: *"The Lord smelled the pleasing aroma and said in his heart: 'Never again will I curse the ground because of man, even though every inclination of his heart is evil from childhood"* (8:21). *The Interpreters Bible* commenting on the verse says, *"Few sentences in Genesis reflect thought so naive as this. God is pleased with the smoke of sacrifice, and He began to feel more warmly disposed. He resigned Himself to recognize that the heart of man is just about hopeless. It has been evil from his youth. So the only thing to do is to accept the situation and not put any dependency upon the possibility of correcting matters by another flood. There is something to be credited of humanity in the person of Noah, and perhaps that is all God can expect"* (p. 547).

The Lord was so deeply moved by the sincerity of this single man that He vowed never to destroy the world again by a flood. Such emotion was not mere maudlin sentiment from a doting father toward his helpless child. A thousand times no! Noah touched God by his faith and obedience, bringing hope to a hopeless world.

We must not underestimate the power of one person who aligns himself with the will and purposes of God. One person can make a difference in the world. Noah changed the course of human history, both literally and spiritually. True, a person may indeed be pitiful; a person may indeed be hopeless. But just let him believe God! Just let him begin

Part I

to worship God! A believing man is a powerful man. A worshiping man is a powerful.

Faith and worship connect impotent man with the omnipotent God. And no man that is in touch with God is without hope. One man and his God; ponder the awesome potential of such combination!

Stay here with me a little while longer! I can't drop the point just yet. If there is but one man who is willing to walk with God, there is hope. We might do well to note that we are here dealing with worship. It's the way that Noah worshiped God that made the difference. For nothing brings God closer to man than worship, especially if it is sincere and sacrificial. And no one can deny that Noah's act of worship here is sincere and sacrificial! Never mind man's hopelessness; think of the profound difference that you and your God could make if you were willing to submit yourself to His divine mandate, if you were willing to put God first in all things, if nothing that you have was too good for Him.

It may be said, new found love softens the heart. It is also said, **"the way to a man's heart is through his belly." Not with God! The way to God's heart is through true worship and true sacrifice.** So moved was God by Noah's act of worship and sacrifice that like a young lover, He was willing to vow. And vow He did: *"As long as the earth endures, seedtime and harvest, cold and heat, summer and winter, day and night will not cease"* (v. 22). Doesn't this sound like the heart of someone running away with love? And in some way it is! It is the divine response to worship, but not mere worship. It is the quality of the worship: *pleasing- aroma worship, which went straight to the nostrils of God. No one could stop it, because it was pure and true worship. Such act of worship changed the course of history. Such act*

A Call to Covenant Relationship

of worship today can change a town, change a city, change a country, and even change our world. God delights in his children's worship of him (Eph. 5:2; Phil. 4: 18).

Noah worshiped God, giving of the best that he had to offer, giving out of the limited supply of what he had. Is it any wonder God showed such respect to the man Noah? God had chosen the right man with whom to make a covenant, a man that effectively and sincerely worshiped Him, a man of faith, a man who was willing to make a supreme sacrifice in honor of his God. Only with such a person will God make his covenant today.

Look a little further, and see what God promised as a result of Noah's single act of worship: *"As long as the earth endures, seedtime and harvest, cold and heat, summer and winter, day and night will never cease."* Never again will God smite the earth, destroying it as he had done before. Instead, the natural order will continue carrying out God's purposes for humanity.

Have you ever thought that our world could not continue without the seasonal alternations of nature! *"Rightly, these alternations of nature are reckoned as the beneficent gifts of God. The great aspects of nature are not monotonous, but neither are they capricious. One can know what is coming next. The longest day will be followed by the restful quiet of the dark, and every night can look forward to another dawn. When winter comes the spring and summer will be not far behind. If there is seedtime, there will be harvest too. There are beauty and stimulus in this unfailing rhythm. Life must respond in different ways to the ebb and flow of light and darkness, cold and heat"* **(Interpreter's Bible, p. 548).**

It is this, then, that forms the basis for a covenant relationship with God. From this time forth, **God wishes for no more**

Part I

dating. No more courting. No more mate selecting. He wants covenant—a permanent relationship. For in a permanent relationship—marriage—neither partner will withhold anything from the other. Nor is the relationship conditional.

Difference Between Covenant and Promise

Part II

As we mentioned earlier, the word covenant is used for the first time in the Bible in Genesis 6:18: *"But I will establish my covenant with you, and you will enter the ark—you and your sons and your wife and your son's wives with you."* We also explained the difference between a covenant and a promise. Now, I'd like to develop that further.

The marriage relationship, of which courtship is a necessary preliminary, provides the context in which covenant is being examined. Covenant bespeaks a permanent agreement. So does marriage! God is always in search of people with whom He can establish a permanent relationship. A problem we face is that some people seem content to remain in a courting mode permanently. They are unwilling to make the permanent commitment that marriage demands. Courting affords them contact without commitment, fun with freedom.

Commitment is the soul of a covenant relationship. That type of relationship Jesus graphically defined for his disciples (Matt. 16:24-26). To that relationship He invited his wavering disciples: *"If anyone would come after me, he must deny himself and take up his cross and follow Me"* (Matt. 16:24).

Peter did not quite seem to grasp the fact that Christ is an all-or-none Proposition. He later found out the hard way. Jesus having told His disciples that He was going to Jerusalem where wicked men would arrest and crucify Him, in hasty impetuosity, Peter began to rebuke Jesus and assured Him, *"This shall never happen to you"* (Matt. 16:22). It was this statement that triggered the Master's solemn reply, *"If anyone would come after me, he must deny himself and take up his cross and follow Me...."* (Matt. 16:24). Jesus is saying to us, as he did to Peter and the rest of the disciples, ninety-nine-and-a-half percent commitment won't do. We've got to go the whole way. Total commitment is what Jesus is looking for.

Total commitment is what I call covenant relationship. That's what I call going from courtship to marriage.

Let's go back to Genesis 8 and pick up the story of Noah. Reporting on life some 150 days after the deluge, verse 1 says, *"And God remembered Noah,"* the man with whom He promised He would make a covenant (Gen. 6:18). Once God has established a covenant with you, He will remember you no matter how long it takes to fulfill it.

God will not forget you out in life's floods. He will not leave you or forsake you. That's the understanding that David came to when he said in Psalm 23, *"Yea though I walk through the valley of the shadow of death I will fear no evil, for thou art with me thy rod and thy staff they comfort me"* (v. 4).

God remembered Noah. Noah had become his soul mate. And God did not merely make a promise with him; he made a covenant! That difference dictated the course of the relationship: covenant.

No one can make a covenant with you and walk away and forget you. The covenant won't let him. That's the nature of a covenant. If you carry the passport of a country, however you became a citizen, whether by birth or by naturalization, the issuing country has formed an irrevocable contract with you. If by chance you were taken hostage by another country, the issuing country would be obliged to try to bring you to safety at all costs. So it is with God! Once He has covenanted with you, no matter where you are He will come to your aid in honor of his covenant commitment. You may be in a far off country, as Abraham was when famine led him to Egypt (Gen 12:10-20). Just as God protected Abraham's wife Sarai from Pharaoh by sending a plague upon Pharaoh's household, so God will be at your side. Let this truth be your anchor by day and polestar by night.

You may be on Mt. Ararat, surrounded by the floodwaters of life. God will remember you, his covenant partner. Yes, you may be in a violent storm in the midst of the sea as Jesus' disciples were (Mk. 6:45-52; Jn. 8:16-21). Jesus will come walking on the water, as he did with the disciples, if that's what it will take to rescue and comfort. The heavenly covenant passport you carry guarantees it.

You may be on a barren, desolate island of Patmos, as John was (Rev. 1:9-16); the Lord will come to you. You may even be in the valley of the shadow of death (Ps. 23:4). Remember the words of the psalmist, *"Even though I walk through the valley of the shadow of death, I will fear no evil, for you are with me; your rod and your staff, they comfort me."* Again the psalmist David declares confidently, *"Where can I go from your Spirit? Where can I flee from your presence? . . . If*

Difference Between Covenant and Promise

I make my bed in the depths [hell], *you are there. If I rise on the wings of the dawn* [east], *if I settle on the far side of the sea* [west], *even there your hand will guide me, your right hand will hold me fast"* (Ps. 139:8-10). If you are a citizen of heaven, if you are God's covenant child, you are never alone—no never, never alone. God promised never to leave you, never to leave you alone!

I can think of nothing that puts this into perspective any better than the poem **"Footprints."**

"One night I dreamed I was walking along the beach with the Lord. Many scenes from my life flashed across the sky. In each scene I noticed footprints in the sand. Sometimes there were two sets of footprints, other times there was only one. This bothered me because I noted that during the low periods of my life when I was suffering from anguish, sorrow, or defeat, I could see only one set of footprints, so I said to the Lord, 'You promised me, Lord, that if I followed you, you would walk with me always. But I have noticed that during the most trying periods of my life there has been only one set of footprints in the sand. Why, when I needed you most, you have not been there?' The Lord replied, 'The times when you have seen only one set of footprints, my child, is when I carried you.'"

How true are the words of the song, "Oh never alone, oh never alone. He promised never to leave me, never to leave me alone."

What is it about a love relationship that causes you to remember the object of your love no matter how far or how long you've been separated. No ocean is large enough to exceed the stretching reach of the cord of love. No distance is too far to diminish the pull of love. No weather is too

Part II

cold to quench love's fire. Love will remain attached to its object. Love will find a way to be with its object. How well John 3:16 depicts God's love for us: *"For God so loved the world that He gave His only begotten Son."* That's the nature of love. It will not stop short, it will not cease, it will not rest until it has found its object. James Rowe expresses this well in song: **"Love lifted me! Love lifted me! When nothing else could help, love lifted me."**

A few years ago a lady showed up at our door. She was from Nigeria. Soon after her tribal marriage five years earlier, Emily's husband left for the U.S.A. to study with the intention of having her join him soon after. But things did not turn out the way they had hoped. Getting a visa for her proved much more difficult than he had anticipated. During this long separation, love never gave up. It continued to seek its object.

Not knowing a single soul on the Island, one day Emily, carrying only a suitcase, arrived in Jamaica. All she knew about Jamaica was that its government turns back no one from another black country. Showing her diplomatic passport to an immigration officer, she was asked the reason for her visit to Jamaica. *"I don't know,"* was her reply. *"And who do you know on the Island?" "No one,"* came the answer. *"Where are you going to stay?"* asked the immigration officer. *"I have no where to go, but I'm a Christian. Do you know any Christian person anywhere?"*

Luckily, someone at the Immigration knew the Rev. Dr. F. Beason. *"Dr. Beason, we have a woman here at the airport all the way from Nigeria. She says she knows no one on the Island, has no money, but has come to Jamaica expecting that she will find some Christian who will take her in. You are the only one we know that we can readily call on. Can you come and get her?"*

Difference Between Covenant and Promise

Confused by everything, but driven by the conviction that a fellow Christian was in desperate need, Dr. Beason went to the airport and picked her up. One of the sisters of the church graciously provided her accommodation. A trained history teacher, Emily soon found a job by which she could take care of some of her basic needs.

Denied a visa to enter the U.S.A. by the U. S. Immigration, with an unrelenting determination, Emily turned her gaze to Canada. She had come to believe that if she got to Canada, she would be nearer to the object of her love. One day I got a call from Jamaica: *"Hello, George. This is Beason. I have a lady here from Nigeria who has been visiting Jamaica for several months. She wants to visit Canada. Do you think you can help her?"* The story of Emily's plight and the tenacity of her love moved me to tears. Feeling secure in the friendship and judgment of a long-time friend, I agreed to receive her.

Emily spent six months with us, all the time doing everything in her power to reach her husband in America. After many failed attempts, one day she left home, giving us very little information. She did not return home that night, which caused us great concern. About two days later I got a telephone call from Emily in which she promptly informed us that she was with her husband. Within a week I received an invitation to their wedding, undertaken to satisfy legal requirements in America. Emily could now rest. She was now with the one her longing heart had been searching for. Never in my life have I seen a love so unyielding and so unfading.

God's covenant love is even stronger and more unrelenting than that of Emily. One hundred and fifty days had passed since the flood inundated the earth, *"but God remembered*

Part II

Noah." God never forgets His own. Oh no, never! Nor should we forget God when the covenant is tested by harsh realities.

Both the flood and its consequences, negative and positive, were designed by God. Noah recognized that. At the end of it all, rather than turn from God, Noah worshiped God. Adversity made him better, not bitter. Noah's altar was no tribute to fate for contriving his escape from disaster. Noah was not thanking some idol god for the good fortune of his survival. No, he knew the origin of all the events that preceded the flood. He was in touch with God Almighty from the first nail to the first drop of rain.

If the blind forces of nature had brought about the flood, and if Noah had planned his own escape as a result of his own premonitions and self-invented precautions, the outcome would never have led to an altar and sacrifice made to God. Nor would it have issued into worship and a vow to the Almighty. Noah's life was governed by covenant. He knew the Person and principle of covenant relationship.

Noah had a vital relationship with God. God was faithful to him, and he was faithful to God. Idiotic as it seemed that a man would build a boat and no water on which to sail it, and to believe rain would fall from the sky when none had ever fallen before is proof of covenant love. Covenanters usually trust each other. Have you got a covenant with God?

Again, let us look where the Ark rested—on Mt. Ararat—one of the highest mountain peaks in the land of Armenia straight north of Nineveh. The Ark did not come to rest in the slush of the valley. If there is ever a flood in your life and you are looking for a place to perch, be sure it is the top of a mountain or you run the risk of winding up in the slush of the valley.

Difference Between Covenant and Promise

There is something marvelous about mountains in Scripture that evokes the image of "lovers' hill." God loves to meet his people on the mountains. It was on a mountain that He met with Moses and commissioned him to deliver His people out of Egyptian bondage (Exod. 3:1). It was on Mount Sinai that God met with Moses to give him the law (Exod. 19). It was on Mount Carmel that He met with Elijah (1Kings 18:21-40). On Mount Moriah it was that God met with Abraham and bade him offer his only son (Gen. 22:2). Jesus often entered into His deepest conversations with the disciples on a mountain (e.g., Mount of Beatitude in Matt. 5-7), and it was from the Mount of Olives that He ascended to His Father (Acts 1:12).

There might well be more to the mountain than meets the eye. It is here that the air is purest, the sight is keenest, and your life is safest. From here you can see the farthest and hear the clearest. From the mountaintop, it is easy for a man to see the course that the events of life are taking, perceive the inevitable consequences of sin, and thus take appropriate remedial action. If God's got you on a mountaintop, enjoy its wonder and grandeur. As you peer through your binoculars and scan the distant scenes, also take a look at the devastation of sin, then take the necessary action lest you fall into a similar or worse predicament.

Mock not as they did in Noah's day, because history can make it no plainer that when man persists in evil, it becomes an offense to God and a peril to the well-being of the world. That's about where we are now. Evil is so rampant that you can smell it in the air. So prevalent is wickedness that wrong is right, black is white, and light is darkness. Children are adult, women are fathers and fathers are mothers, the victimized is wrong and the perpetrator is right.

Part II

Where are we going? The seniors of our society are mugged, our children, whom we should guard with our lives, are objects of pornographic pictures. Men have become idols of worship. Sport figures draw more crowds than Billy Graham and Benny Hinn. Lord, help us to truly see earth's need from the lofty height of Mount Ararat. The vision once grasped will change our lives and destinies. Small wonder Noah became a preacher of righteousness.

It was from this highest vantage point (Ararat) that mankind got a second chance at life. Loving Father that He is, God will always give you the best chance to start over. He will set your feet upon the rock to stay, plant your feet on solid ground.

If you want to go to the despair of the valley, that's your choice; but God will always give you the best chance to start over on the mountaintop. What a beautiful chance He gives to all of us, lifting us from the valley and putting us on the mountaintop from which we can take wings and fly away into a new life with God, into a new life in the Spirit. Let's take it, weary children!

If you are on the mountaintop, take advantage of it. Look out from your place of rest, and view the land below. If you ever have to go down to the valley, be sure that the floodwaters have abated. And make certain the Lord is with you! The valley might have all the lilies, the springs of cool clear water, all the trees with bountiful shades and beautiful flowers, but they provide little pleasure or satisfaction if the Lord is not with you.

The floodwaters have now abated. The darkness is past. Dry land has returned. Noah and his precious cargo have exited the Ark. Life is about to begin anew. God's covenant sign to Noah that the past will never again return and that a

Difference Between Covenant and Promise

bright future looms on the horizon is a rainbow. *"And God said, 'This is the sign of the covenant I am making between me and you and every living creature with you . . . . I have set my rainbow in the clouds, and it will be the sign of the covenant between me and the earth' "* (Gen. 9:12-13). Verses 14-16 explain the significance of the rainbow. It's a token that God will never again destroy the earth with a flood.

How interesting and pertinent are these verses to our real life relationships. The first thing a person to whom you promise your love is looking for is a "token." Words alone are not enough! You can breathe out fancy words all you want; the silliest of women is not listening till you give her a token of your love. You may have walked in the garden in the cool of the day and picked a rose and stuck it in her hair. You may have whispered a thousand sweet words in her ear. Still she waits for the token. A token signifies real interest in a serious relationship. It is a visible, tangible symbol of love.

The rainbow was God's "token" to Noah. It symbolized commitment. It betokened a serious relationship together in the future.

Covenant—A Binding Relationship

Part III

By way of reminder, this topic is set in the context of courtship and marriage. The reason is its vital link between the family, worship and its relationship to the church. It is also worth remembering the essential difference between a promise and a covenant. **A promise creates expectation. A covenant does more: it creates a binding contract.** Besides, with a promise one partner is active and the other passive—the benefactor promises and the beneficiary simply accepts. That is why, a transaction no matter how strong, once entered into based merely on a promise, can be broken at anytime. Not so with a covenant!

A **covenant is another matter all together.** In order to create a covenant, two persons must be active. Both must sign, swear, or shed blood in consideration of the agreement to be entered into. A covenant establishes a permanent agreement, and both parties must duly enter into it. What is also important about a covenant is that it often goes beyond the lives of the covenanters, bearing implication and

Covenant—A Binding Relationship

consequence even for succeeding generations. Marriage illustrates this fact. We in society insist on a marital contract. Love between two people is not enough. That love must be sealed by a legal agreement. That legal agreement obligates each partner to certain responsibilities.

There are two cases in point in Canada that illustrate the nature of covenant. In the first case, shortly after the marriage, the wife became crippled. As a result, the husband divorced her. Not being able to support herself, she sued him for support after they had been divorced for years. Guess what! Her request was granted, based on the marriage vow: "for better, for worse."

In the second case, the wife divorced her husband because he was an alcoholic. Unable to support himself because of his alcoholism, he sued his former wife for support. Guess what! His request was granted, based on the same grounds. That's the nature of contract or covenant!

When one is single, no one can legally lay claim to what he or she has based solely on a verbal agreement or a platonic relationship. Marriage drastically changes that! In marriage, all that the husband possesses by a stroke of the pen becomes the wife's and all that the wife possesses becomes the property of the husband. And, if for any reason, misfortune should be the lot of either party moments after vowing and signing the bond, the one must forever carry the name and thereby bear all the misfortune or own all the fortune of the other.

No one can contest or deprive you based on the brevity of the relationship. For many Christians, Jesus granting the thief on the cross paradise all so suddenly (*"Today you will be with me in paradise,"* Luke 23:39, *NIV*) is problematic. Sometimes, members of the kingdom become a little jealous

Part III

when a new convert is born into the church and shortly thereafter begins to reap as many benefits as those who have been there a long time. Don't be alarmed! It's not how long you have been with Christ; it's whether or not the covenant has been signed. It's not the length of time of the relationship that matters. It's the contract. It's a matter of whether or not it has been signed and sealed!

We need to understand that in eternity past, when God asked, **"Who will go and die for the world?"** Jesus answered, **"I will go."** That decision constituted a contract that included anyone who would come to Him in faith, anywhere, anyhow, anytime. When Jesus said on the cross, *"It is finished"* (John 19:30, *NIV*), **that was the signing of the eternal contract that sealed the covenant relationship and gave us legal right to our inheritance.** Hence, if you see a drunk coming out of the gutters and into the pulpit, that is why. If you see a prostitute coming off the streets and into the church choir, that is why. Yea, if you see a murderer coming off death row and into the high services of the church, that is why. It is all due to the signing of the eternal contract.

It may be said, **"what the blood covenant did for Israel and ancient man, the pen and ink does for us."** If you like, when time has passed and memory has faded; when the hips and the waist have changed and the heart has grown cold; when the hair has grown silver and the sight has grown dim, **the covenant stands fast**.

Have you signed your covenant with God, yet? Have you talked with your God closely? Has your relationship been consolidated? The songwriter asks, **"How long has it been since you talked with the Lord and told Him your heart's hidden secret?"**

Covenant—A Binding Relationship

In order to put this in perspective let's contemplate an actual marriage contract.

"**Dearly beloved, we are gathered here together in the sight of God and in the presence of these witnesses, to join together this man and this woman in Holy matrimony. It is therefore not to be entered into unadvisedly, but reverently and discretely, and in the fear of God. Into this holy estate these two persons come now to be joined. If anyone can show just cause why they may not be lawfully joined together- let him now state or forever hereafter, hold his peace. I require and charge you both, as you stand in the presence of God, before whom the secrets of all hearts are disclosed, that having duly considered the holy COVENANT you are about to make, you now declare before this company your pledge of FAITH each to the other....**"

Have you ever wondered why this is said? It is a perfect preamble, because two people are about to enter into a permanent covenant. Watch how the foregone statement seems to extricate itself from the weakness of the flesh, human thought and ideology, and moves into the realm of the permanent and timeless: "**let him now state or forever hereafter, hold his peace.**" "**State now**" has a sense of the present, hence it is human. It is existential, compared to "**forever hereafter, hold his peace.**" Just in case you missed the emphasis, it is the "**forever**" that's the nature of covenant as opposed to "promise."

If no one voices disapproval, the wedding begins in earnest: "**Jack, will you have Jill to be your wedded wife, to have and to hold, from this day forward, for better for worse, for richer for poorer, in sickness and in health, to love and to cherish, till death us do part?**" Jack responds, "I

will!" Note, responding in the affirmative is very important. Without it the wedding comes to an abrupt end. **"Why?"** you may ask. Simply because he is entering into a covenant, which requires the active involvement of two participants. Remember, a covenant is not just a promise; it is a permanent contract.

The said vow must be repeated by Jill, in the same manner, and requires the very same response: **"I will!"** After all, it is a covenant, not just a promise. In further fulfilling the requirements of the wedding covenant of mutual commitment, both parties must respond **"I do."** If either party fails to answer, **"I do!"** The wedding again comes to an abrupt end.

In our society, the marriage covenant is further formalized by the giving and receiving of a ring or rings—a tradition not to be taken lightly. A ring publicly declares that one has become the soul mate of another. Jesus, putting this in the perspective of discipleship said, *"No servant can serve two masters. Either he will hate the one and love the other, or he will be devoted to the one and despise the other. You cannot serve both God and Money"* (Luke 16:13, *NIV*).

Moses, coming down from Mount Sinai, similarly called attention to this exclusive relationship between God and Israel when addressing the people who had fallen into idolatry: *" Whoever is for the Lord, come to me"* (Exod. 32:26, *NIV*). If you feel I'm too much of a Bible puncher, listen to a line from a popular song of the world that echoes the folly of conjugal disloyalty: **"falling in love with two lovers, acting like a fool."** What I'm trying to say is, there must be absolute commitment and loyalty between covenanting partners.

Paul says, *"Therefore, if anyone is in Christ, he is a new creation; old things have passed away; behold, all things have become new"* (2 Cor. 5:17, *NKJV*). May we substitute **"new"** with **"different?"** What is said of the relationship between Christ and the believer may be applied to the couple in marriage. That covenant relationship changes one of the most fundamental pronouns in the English language: "I" or "me." From the moment one answers "I do," the "I" is changed to "we" and "me" to "us."

The Ring

Let us go back to Jack and Jill to whom we referred earlier. In order to let the world know that they are serious about their nuptial agreement, they brought a ring as a public seal and token. The ring is a permanent token of their endless, abiding, mutual love—an outward and visible sign of an inward and spiritual grace, signifying to all the uniting of this man and this woman in holy matrimony, through the church of our Lord Jesus Christ.

So, let us present the ring. Jack, please repeat after me, **"In token and pledge of our constant faith and abiding love, with this ring I thee wed, in the name of the Father and of the Son, and of the Holy Ghost."** Jill, will you now repeat after me, **"In token and pledge of our constant faith and abiding love, with this ring I thee wed, in the name of the Father and of the Son, and of the Holy Ghost."** Both Jack and Jill must say the same thing in order for it to be a covenant, and a covenant is necessary in such an undertaking. As you know, sometimes sly intruders—even old flames of past times—can be daring, willing to stake a claim if given half a chance. But like a flag waving in the brisk breeze, the ring announces to old acquaintances and all that things are different now. A covenant relationship has been established between Jack and Jill.

Part III

Now that we have come this far, we might as well complete the transaction. For it appears to me that the groom is anxious to kiss the bride. **"For as much as Jack and Jill have consented together in holy wedlock, and have witnessed the same before God and this company, and to this have pledged their faith each to the other and have declared the same by joining hands and by the giving and receiving of rings, I pronounce that they are husband and wife together! Whom therefore God has joined together let no man put asunder, amen!"** Don't forget, this is all about "covenant," not a wedding.

Once you have formed a covenant, no one should come between you and your covenant partner. What is true of the covenant of marriage is also true of the covenant of church membership. Sadly, however, there are many Christians who have joined the church, but are still looking at the world from the corner of one eye, sometimes even intimating that they were better off in the world than they are in the church. My friend, when you were being accepted into membership, you vowed **"for better for worse."** You made a covenant. **A covenant is not a promise; nor is it a mere contract**, as most contracts are drafted. **It is a permanent agreement with very serious consequences, if violated.** You and the church exchanged rings, just as Jack and Jill did.

The kissing of the Bride

I often wonder why we call for the kissing of the bride at the close of the wedding. I've learned that its purpose is more than painting an image of romance and eliciting laughter from the audience. It serves as the final public consummation of the contract.

Earlier on, Jack and Jill repeated the vows verbally and verbatim in front of the whole company, saying out loud, "I

Covenant—A Binding Relationship

will" and **"I do."** Part three of the wedding vow says, **"In as much as Jack and Jill have consented together, by the holding of hands and the giving and receiving of rings, I now pronounce you man and wife together. Whom therefore God has joined together, let no man put asunder."**

Most of the wedding ceremony up to this point deals with verbal intentions and agreements. But verbal acquiescence and assent is not enough. The bond must be physically and publicly sealed and signed. A kiss does that. Jesus might well have told us that by his mere intention to give His life for us would be enough for our redemption. But, no! He must go to the old rugged cross.

Up until now, the bride may or may not have yet been kissed. Whether she has been or not, it's high time for the groom to publicly kiss his bride. Jack, you may now kiss the bride!

A kiss is an expression of love. In the context of marriage, it symbolizes love and a covenant relationship. In the Bible, kissing is sometimes related to worship or homage. Psalm 2:12 says, *"Kiss the son* [Son of God, Jesus] *lest he be angry."* Here the rulers of the earth are summoned to worship or do homage to the Son of God, lest they become the objects of his wrathful displeasure. An act of worship is clearly evident in Luke 7:37-38, where a penitent prostitute kisses the feet of Jesus and anoints them with fragrant oil.

In the West, kissing largely has a very personal if not private connotation, and often also a sexual one. That is why men shake hands and, at best, embrace. But in the East, two men meeting greet each other with a double kiss—one on each cheek. And, of course, if you were in Russia, you would get one on each cheek and one on the mouth.

Kissing in the Bible captures the social and cultural function of that custom as practiced in the Middle East, which includes respect, fellowship, and affection. When applied to deity, however, it betokens worship. Whether applied to the social or the religious function, what is true of both is that kissing can be done only to another person in close proximity.

If our discourse is to be understood, this aspect must be clearly grasped. "Getting close" is a term that is so often used in regards to worship. **We worship to get close, and we get close so that we can worship**. That is why there is something inseparable between courtship, marriage and worship. Little wonder Paul uses marriage to exemplify Christ's relationship to the church (Eph. 6.20-30).

Normally, you don't walk up to a stranger and pop a kiss on them, because that act is suggestive of "familiarity." Kissing is reserved for someone you know well, and someone who knows you well. In a word, that "someone" has to earn the right to do so. **So, also, a close personal relationship with God belongs to those who have come into covenant relationship with Him.**

God is calling the church to a "kissing" distance with Him. He is beckoning each of us to a "kissing" relationship with Him—a relationship in which you can kiss Him on both cheeks. Enoch walked so closely with God that God took him away to Himself (Gen. 5:24). He took him into an exclusive relationship like He had with Adam before the fall (Gen. 3), and the relationship we will have when our restoration is complete.

Watch Jesus as He crisscrosses Palestine beckoning to different ones to a meaningful relationship. "*Come to me; all you who labor and are heavy laden, and I will give you rest*" is his word of invitation (Matt. 11:28, *NKJV*). One day He is found at a wedding (John 2), the next at the seashore, and next at some synagogue. One day takes him to the pool of

Covenant—A Binding Relationship

Bethesda, the next to the countryside, and the next to the city. Wherever you find Him, good chances are He is calling someone to Himself. Even as He completes His redemptive work on Calvary's cross, dying though He is, He calls a dying thief to Himself: *"Today you will be with me in paradise"* (Luke 23:43, *NIV*).

God desires to be in a kissing relationship with us. And it does not matter who you are, where you are from, what your station in life is. If He finds you to be willing to heed His voice, you are the person He is looking for.

After the Honeymoon

Part IV

But *I will establish my covenant with you, and you will enter the ark—you and your sons and your wife and your sons' wives with you"* **(Gen. 6:18).**

Marriage is probably one of the best ways modern society may understand the concept of biblical covenant, and indeed, marriage is a context in which the very essence of covenant is played out. Because the Church is the Bride of Christ, implications of biblical covenant apply to that relationship. We must always bear in mind, as explained earlier, that a covenant is greater than a promise or even a conventional contract.

As you might recall, in part three we talked about marriage. As a matter of fact, we looked at an actual marriage contract and had Jack and Jill repeat their vows. Now, let me pose a question. What happens after a wedding? In western culture, we have a period called the honeymoon—a custom with an ancient and somewhat savage background.

In ancient times, it was customary among the northern nations of Europe for newly married couples to drink

After the Honeymoon

milheglin or mead—a kind of wine made from honey—for about thirty days after the marriage. This was particularly true of the periods when women often became brides through capture or marriages in which both partners eloped and went into hiding to get married. Antiquarians believe the custom of couples drinking milheglin during this time was termed "honey month," honeymoon being the modern derivation.

What is the purpose of the honeymoon? In western customs the honeymoon period seems to be a time when newlyweds get away from the hustle and bustle of life's daily routine in order to get to know each other better. During this time, the bride needs to hear only the sweet voice of the groom whispering in her ear and to feel the tender touch of his hand gently sweeping across her body. You cannot get to know another person by dating alone. There is an old adage that says, **"To see me and to live with me are two different things."**

What I'm trying to say is, the honeymoon is a time newlyweds get to know each other in a way they cannot otherwise. It is a time to consolidate all that has preceded it. It is a time to nurture the metamorphosis that has begun during courtship. It is a time for the merging of minds, hearts and will and deepening of spirits. This is what I call the metamorphosis of beings.

If you are one who observes human behavior, you can almost always easily spot a newly married couple. They are constantly in each other's company. They walk holding hands, and they can hardly take their eyes off each other. If they are in the same house, you will rarely get them to be in separate rooms. "Why?" you may ask. They are in the process of becoming one. Can you imagine your best friends just returning from their honeymoon looking sour,

Part IV

walking at a distance from each other? That would be most distressing, wouldn't you say?

The newly-wed woman wants the world to know she has achieved one of society's most desired statuses. One way of making it known is to wave the ring finger in the wind for everyone to see. Even more important to her is the new name she now shares.

Nowhere does a name have more profound significance than in the world of the Bible. As a matter of fact, the same way genes carry genetic information, so also a name in the biblical world carried a considerable amount of information about its bearer. Do you remember Jacob, whose name means **"supplanter?"** After he wrestled with the angel and prevailed, his name was changed from Jacob to Israel—**"a prince"** or **"one having power with God"** (Gen. 32: 28). Note that with the change of name came a change of character. And a change of name causes a change of outlook on life. It changes your station in life, your frame of reference, and your fortune.

No story more clearly exemplifies the power of a name change than the story of Ruth. As you know, the story did not start with Ruth, but with Elimelech of Bethlehem Judah and his family (Ruth 1.2). Out of fear for his economic well-being, he left Bethlehem and went to Moab, a forbidden land, in search of greener pastures. While in the land of Moab, both of his sons, Mahlon and Chilion married Moabite women. Within ten years, Elimelech and his sons died in the land of Moab.

Ravished by misfortune, after ten years in Moab Elimelech's widow, Naomi, decided to cut her losses, dry her tears, lick her wounds, bundle up what was left, and go home to Bethlehem, **"the house of bread,"** from whence she came. Returning crestfallen to her community, she refused to be called Naomi, a name that suggests **"pleasantness."** *"Call me no more Naomi, but call me 'Marah'"*—**"bitter,"** she bemoaned (Ruth 1:19, 20).

A change of name in the covenant of marriage is even more powerful. Just pretend that border crossings and passports existed at the time of Naomi. Picture three single women, Naomi and her two Moabite daughters-in-law, with their meager belongings trekking north from Moab, up the eastern side of the Jordan, perhaps fording the river north of Gilgal, then going west toward Jerusalem and then southwest towards Bethlehem.

Imagine standing at the border where you can see them as they approach the custom officer. Visualize the pathos, the wrenching human drama that will transpire. Ten years of life's emotional cords are about to be violently severed. Watch them as they try to part company. *"And Naomi said to her two daughters-in-law, 'Go, return each to her mother's house. The Lord deal kindly with you, as you have dealt with the dead and with me'"* (Ruth 1:8).

Well, the two daughters-in-law try to hang on to ten years of history—and chances are they were the best ten years of their lives, the deaths of their husbands bringing the only possible blight to their happiness. They want to follow their mother-in-law home. But Naomi, the matriarch, insists: *"Turn back, my daughters, go—for I am too old to have a husband"* (1:12) with whom I may have sons for you to marry. **"Go home; it's all over. There is no future for you in Bethlehem."** That's what Naomi is saying. Her persuasiveness gets the better of Orpah, and she goes back, disappearing into the shadows of oblivion, never to be mentioned in Biblical history again.

Part IV

But that is not how the story ends. When Naomi comes to Ruth, she is faced with a different kettle of fish. Nothing she tries on her works. She will not be moved. A long, intense dialogue ensues. "**My mind is made up, Bethlehem is home for me, as it is for you, and that's the way it's going to be,**" Ruth tells her mother-in-law (1: 16).

"You must go back, your sister is leaving you. Go, catch up with her; Palestine is a foreign land with a foreign people; you can't just enter into it like that. Furthermore, our way of life is different. Our worship is different, even the foods we eat are different. You must go back. Besides, you need a passport to go into Palestine," Naomi implores. "Mother I carried my passport. I had made up my mind a long time ago that I was not going to return from following you," Ruth replies.

"Oh, did you? But that does not help, Ruth. Your passport will show that you are of Moabite descent." "Yes, mother, but aren't you forgetting something?" "What might that be, Ruth?" "You are forgetting that I was married to your son, Mahlon." "So!" Naomi retorts, staring at her quizzically. "So, my name has been changed from that of a Moabite to that of an Israelite. How can they turn me back? Mother, my married name gives me the rights to enter into your country unhindered." "Well, Ruth, I don't know about that, but since you insist, let's try, " Naomi acquiesces.

Mark them as they stand in the line, the face of Naomi registering apprehension. The custom officer takes a quick glance at them as they get nearer to him. Finally, it's their turn. The custom officer beckons them to come, reaching out for their passport. He quickly fingers through Naomi's and waves her by. He looks curiously at Ruth and then at her passport. "**Everything about her seems so different,**

After the Honeymoon

except the name," he says to himself. He repeats the process, scanning the passport then Ruth. Convinced that she is a foreigner, he asks her, **"Who are you, and where are you going?"** "I was born in Moab, and married to a Bethlehemite named Mahlon." "How long is your visit?" **"I'm not visiting. I'm going to live with my mother-in-law, Naomi, in Bethlehem." "She is with me!"** Naomi interrupts.

"I cannot let you in. The name "Mahlon" signifies "weakness," and I cannot let you in on a name like that. Where is your husband anyway?" the officer queries. "He is dead. This is my mother-in-law."

"Sir," Ruth implores passionately, **"Mahlon was the son of Elimelech,"** which means **"my God is king."** The officer recognizes the name and acknowledges the power of it: **"Elimelech"—"my God is king."** Clouds of despair suddenly give way to beams of sunshine of hope. **"Do you accept this name?"** the officer asks teasingly. **"Of course. It's my name,"** Ruth ejaculates. **"Then welcome to your new country,"** comes the sweet retort.

The awesome power represented in the covenant of marriage! Soon this Moabitess would meet her redeemer, Boaz, a kinsman of Naomi, who would, by marriage, change everything in her life—a change that would affect both her present and her future; a change that would affect her life through eternity.

Ruth went from being an outsider to being an insider, from the outdoors to the indoors. She went from emptiness to fullness, from poverty to plenty, from weakness to greatness, and from misfortune to good fortune. Once an unknown Moabite, now Ruth has become a lady of Israel, climbing from skid row to the front row, from the poor house to the penthouse.

Ruth's life exemplifies the truth that participation in the coming kingdom is decided not by blood and birth, but by the conformity of one's life to the will of God, through obedience that comes by faith (Rom. 1: 5). And, indeed, her place in the ancestry of David puts us on notice that all nations and peoples will be represented in the kingdom of David's greater Son.

Like Ruth, I can gratefully sing, **"Look where he brought me from."** My name before conversion was George S. Sinner—yes, **"Sinner,"** and that determined my outlook, my attitude and my fortune. But in conversion, in and during the spiritual metamorphic process, Jesus took away the last name. Crumbling it in His mighty hand, he made a new name out of it and gave it back to me. My name is no longer **"Sinner."** My new name is **"Saint,"** and I do not like anyone calling me by my old name. I want everyone to know that I have a new name, because I am a new man in Christ: *"Therefore if any man be in Christ, he is a new creature: old things are passed away; behold, all things are become new"* (2 Cor. 5:17).

You might not be able to tell how all so suddenly I came from being a sinner to a saint, or how I came from being someone so depraved to someone so blessed. That's because you do not quite understand the power of metamorphosis—a power exemplified in the transformation of a caterpillar into a butterfly. To become a butterfly, a caterpillar first encases itself in a cocoon for a period of time. While there, an extraordinary change takes place, transforming an ugly looking creature into one of the most beautiful and

After the Honeymoon

exquisite creatures on earth. Even the most timid of persons is delighted by the monarch butterfly fluttering in the swift evening breeze, gracefully performing in its beautiful garb a ballet to the music of the wind.

If I might add, it is not only the metamorphosis from caterpillar to butterfly that arrests my imagination, but the fact that the caterpillar, prior to metamorphosing, is influenced by its environment. Only the keen eye can detect the caterpillar on a tomato leaf, for example. Having eaten the green substance, it becomes green. But after it has metamorphosed, the color it emerges with is permanent. Now a butterfly, it is no longer influenced by its environment. If anything, it influences its environment.

You might have been a caterpillar up to now. You might have been tossed by every wind of doctrine. You have looked liked everything around you. But if you are born again, you are no longer a lowly caterpillar; you are a lustrous butterfly that takes on the beauty of heaven's Monarch, Jesus Christ, and flies on the winds of his abundant grace. You've been given a new nature, a new look and a new lift.

Permit me to rewind and pick up on a thought I made earlier about the honeymoon Now that the honeymoon is ended, what next? What do we do after the honeymoon? No matter how beautiful an experience it is, a honeymoon is not meant to last forever. Eternal honeymooners are not to be found in any society—old or new.

After the honeymoon, the couple returns to build a home. Wherever you may have lived up to now, represents a completed chapter in your life. You may have rented. You may have lived in your parents' home, with a friend or relative—wherever or whatever—you now need a place of your own: something to call home.

Part IV

Now that you are married and have returned from the honeymoon, it's home-building time, and whatever the size or condition of the domicile, however small or poorly furnished, it is yours. And you should not want to go back to your former residents, be they family or friends! *"For this reason a man will leave his father and mother and be united to his wife, and they will become one flesh"* (Gen. 2:24, NIV).

If after you are married and have come home to build your home you are still thinking about who and what you have left, it is apparent that you do not understand the process. There is an old West Indian adage that says, *"Mother has, Father has, but blessed is the child that has his own."* Your own might not be anything compared to your family, friend or neighbors, but better a shack that is yours than a mansion that is someone else's.

So also, the newly converted person that has come into a covenant relationship with God must be willing to settle down with him and build a home.

The idea of building a home suggests permanence. It suggests that you have taken the relationship seriously. Some people never seem to unpack after the wedding. That makes it easy for them to be up and away with the first disagreement. As you and I well know, one of the things that makes moving so unpleasant is packing. So, when your luggage is already packed, it makes it so much easier to leave your new home.

So it is with some people, they never settle down with God. They seem to have gone through the dating, the courting, and even the honeymoon. But they never settle down with God. It is time you wave the ring finger and let the would-be intruder know that things have changed. Let them know that you have a new name and a new identity and that you belong to someone new. Often their mind is still on the old boyfriend or girlfriend. But it shouldn't be so. If you have said **"I do"** to God, stay with him. Don't you know that home building takes time and patience?

I am often fascinated by West Indians. I can recall the many couples that got married and moved into a one-room dwelling. Not a one-bedroom house, but a one-room dwelling! Yet, as time went by they kept adding a room at a time to the one room until ten or twenty years later a veritable mansion replaced it. To be sure, there were times when it seemed plans to expand came to a screeching halt, with no movement for years. Then all of a sudden a son, a daughter or a brother, sent in some money from abroad and the building program was on again.

You may have started out small with God, but stay the course. Build on what you have. Length and last you will have a mansion. Keep building with God. One of these days, you will wind up with a mansion. Sometimes the road will be tough even though you are walking with Him. But stay the course. Build with Him. The race is not for the swift or the battle to the strong... (Ecc. 9: 11, *NIV*). A covenant is covenant when it is better and when it is worse. It is covenant in sickness and in health. Stay the course.

Some people are permanent tenants. They like renting. Seething in the inner chambers of their hearts is the fear of responsibility that ownership demands. No bank will lend a large sum of money to a person whose suitcase is always packed. Nor will an employer give a position of importance to a person who flees responsibility.

Part IV

When you put your application for a position or blessing from God, and he finds that your resume reads like a man whose suitcase is always packed, how can you hope for a blessing. In a word, the first time you encounter any resistance or discouragement, you are up and gone out of God's house just like you would be up and gone out of a relationship in which you experience difficulties. It is evidence that you do not quite grasp the concept of covenant.

God's blessing upon your life is a sure sign that God can trust you. Little wonder Jesus says in the parable of the dishonest steward, *"Whosoever can be trusted with very little can also be trusted with much, and whoever is dishonest with very little will also be dishonest with much"* (Luke 16:10). Paul adds, *"Now it is required that those who have been given a trust must prove faithful"* (1 Cor. 4:2). In a word, if God cannot find you to be trustworthy, certain responsibility and prominence will not be given to you.

After the honeymoon is over and house building has taken place, it is time for sharing. The whole intent of marriage is sharing. Nothing is to be hidden in the relationship. Covenant makes sharing necessary—sharing of space, property, and personal information. "I" must become "we." There must be a blending of identities. It would be a pleasant surprise for a wife to be told after several years in marriage, **"Honey, I know I should have told you before, but I wanted to surprise you. I do have a million dollars in a bank in Switzerland, you know."** The wife would perhaps respond, **"How nice, Honey. What other secrets do you need to let me into? What other surprises do I need to know about?"** In a covenant relationship such as marriage there is no room for such behavior. The same is true with the Christian life.

After the Honeymoon

Reciprocity is a necessary context in which covenant is played out. No book in the Bible seems to heighten and highlight the reciprocity of covenant relationship quite like Deuteronomy, whose theme is renewal of the covenant.

The covenant was originally given at Mt. Sinai. The said covenant is now renewed on the plains of Moab in preparation for entry into the Promised Land. After they have wondered in the wilderness for forty years, the Israelites will now learn that the original promises of God still stand, both in the times of blessing when they obeyed Him and in the times of judgment when they sinned against Him and disobeyed his laws.

This is what I find profitable: The covenant was renewed at the gate to the land of promise. It marks the end of the old life, as they know it and the beginning of a new life. But before they can embark upon it, the covenant must be renewed because the first covenant was not made with them but with their parents. And God has no grandchildren, only children! Hence, they had to affirm the covenant for themselves. It is my sense that God has allowed me to proclaim this topic at this time because once more we are at the very entrance to the Promised Land.

The Israelites needed to know that God had formed a covenant relationship, that is, he chose Israel as His soul mate and had married them as a people at Mt. Sinai.

This was the first of many times that He would renew His covenant with Israel and demand that they rededicate themselves to the purpose of God. It was first renewed under Joshua at Shechem (Josh. 24), and again under Ezra (Neh. 8).

The pattern for the renewal of the covenant is set out in the book of Deuteronomy, and includes the following:

Part IV

(1) The people are reminded of what God had done to deliver them out of Egyptian slavery. The mighty acts of God are recalled and the weakness and the helplessness of a pitiful people are contrasted with the mercy of God (Deut. 4:5).

(2) The goodness of God is extolled as the people are reminded of the wonderful land which God has opened up before them (Deut. 6:3).

(3) Israel is challenged to be a "peculiar people" of the Lord, an instrument of redemption for the nations (Deut. 7: 6).

(4) A central place of worship is designated for the tabernacle in the wilderness and, eventually, the temple in Jerusalem (Deut.12: 5-11).

(5) Warnings and exhortations are given to the people, and the solemn duty of keeping the divine law is underlined by the certainty of divine punishment for disobedience. (Deut.12: 5-11).

(6) Finally, each instance of the covenant renewal is exclaimed by a promise of the blessings and rest that would attend their faithful observance of the covenant relationship with God (Deut. 4: 40; 6:13).

It was this concept of covenant that gave Israel a whole new understanding of their history. They saw in it the drama of God's redemptive purpose, and every part of their national life was seen as sacred unto the Lord. And, it was just such an understanding of the renewed covenant that made it possible for the early Christians to interpret the gospel of Jesus Christ as a "new covenant," not one written upon the tables of stone, but one written upon the heart, as Jeremiah promised.

"What is the purpose of all this?" you may ask me. In a word, God's covenant with Israel informs our covenant of marriage and Christian covenant relationship with Christ.

Further, it sets forth the ground rules of covenant of which each covenant partner should be cognizant. A promise can be made in ignorance, not so with a covenant.

Each instance of the covenant renewal was exclaimed by a promise of the blessings that would attend its faithful observance.

"If you fully obey the Lord your God and carefully follow all his commands I give you today, the Lord your God will set you on high, above all the nations in earth. All these blessings will come upon you and accompany you if you obey the Lord your God" (Deut. 28:1 ff., NIV).

"You will be blessed in the city and blessed in the country. The fruit of your womb will be blessed, and the crops of your land and the young of your livestock-the calves of your herd and the lambs of your flocks. Your basket and your kneading trough will be blessed. You will be blessed when you go out and blessed when you come in and blessed when you go out" (Deut. 28:5-6, NIV).

"However, if you do not obey the Lord your God and do not carefully follow all his commands and decrees I am giving you today, all these curses will come upon you and over take you: You will be cursed in the city and cursed in the country. Your basket and your kneading trough will be cursed. The fruit of your womb will be cursed, and the crop of your land, and the calves of your herds and the lambs of your flocks. You will be cursed when you come in and cursed when you go out" (Deut. 28:15-19, NIV).

What an extraordinary challenge that is presented to us in the covenant relationship, and what powerful opportunities of blessings. But if you are not convinced, let's examine the message of "Malachi," a name meaning, **"messenger of Jehovah."**

Part IV

"I have loved you," says the Lord. *"But you ask, "How have you loved us?"*

"Was not Esau Jacob's brother?" the Lord, says. "Yet I loved Jacob, but Esau I have hated, and I have turned his mountains into a waste and left his inheritance to the desert jackals," (Mal. 1:1-2, NIV). What could all this mean except that God wants a relationship with his people similar to that of a marriage relationship.

There is, however, a difference in the approach laid out by Malachi and that found in Deuteronomy. Malachi is not asking for a renewal of the covenant, but rather rebuking the Jews for being unfaithful in the covenant relationship. Hence, he asks, **"How can you say you have a covenant relationship with me and behave like this?"** This is not how people in a covenant relationship behave. A stern warning and threat of destruction is issued if they do not return to covenant relationship. *"Because of you I will rebuke your descendants; I will spread on your faces the offal from your festival sacrifices, and you will be carried off with it. And you will know that I have sent you this abomination that my covenant with Levi may continue,"* says the Lord Almighty **(Mal. 2: 3-4, NIV).**

This is how seriously God takes covenant. Of course, it was the priests to whom these words were directed. God wanted to destroy them, but because the covenant was made with Levi and Levi obeyed Him, He could not totally despise them because of the covenant He had made with their forefather, Levi. It goes to show how good it is to be in a covenant relationship. It works both ways for us. It is a blessing when we walk in the covenant relationship, and protects us when we stray from it. Were it not for the covenant between God and Levi, God would not have

After the Honeymoon

exhorted them to return to the covenant. He would simply have destroyed them from the face of the earth.

Instead, He chided them severely, because they were behaving not like a people in a covenant relationship. They had given polluted things to God. *"A son honors his father,"* says God, *"and a servant his master. If I am a father, where is the honor due me? If I am a master, where is the respect due me?" says the Lord Almighty. "But you ask, "How have we shown contempt for your name?" "You place defiled food on my table...."* **(Mal. 1:6-7, NIV).** God was angry with them not only because they did not behave like covenant people.

The Jews as a people did not eat anything polluted. That being so, giving polluted things to God was the same as giving to Him things that they did not want for themselves. That is why it was so abominable to God. **"When you bring blind animals for sacrifice is that not wrong? When you bring crippled or diseased animals, is that not wrong?"** (2:8, *NIV*).

To add insult to injury, they no longer gave priority to worship, nor cared for the temple. Few things angered God more effectively than abandoning his house (1:13). It was the abandonment of His house that gave rise to the prophecy of the prophet Haggai. So keen is God about his house that He spoke directly to His servant in regards to His house. *"This is what the Lord Almighty says: the people say, "the time has not yet come for the Lord's house to be built."* But while they were saying that, the word of the Lord came to the prophet saying, *"Is it not time for you yourselves to live in your paneled houses, while this house remained in ruin?"* (Hag. 1: 2-3, *NIV*).

"What is so important about the house of the Lord?" you may ask. It is the center of everything. It is the place from which all blessings flow. That is why in olden days, the house of a god was in the middle of the city or village. It was believed everything flowed from it to all parts of the community. Besides, it was where the god met with his people. So, if the house of God is in ruins, God is not able to meet with His people.

Not only did the Jews abandon the house of God; they also robbed God, for which sin they incurred a stern warning. *"I the Lord do not change. So you, O descendants of Jacob, are not destroyed. Ever since the time of your forefathers you have turned from my decrees and have not kept them. Return to me and I will return to you,"* says the Lord Almighty **(Mal. 3:6-7, NIV)**. They had the dare to ask God if indeed they had robbed Him, and how they had turned from Him. **"You have robbed Me,"** God said. *"In tithe and offerings. "You are under a curse"* (Mal. 3.8-9, *NIV*).

In a word, if God did not operate by eternal principles, if He were able to change His covenant, He could have changed His mind and destroyed them. But His covenant would not allow him. Then why is He so angry? Why not? Why would anyone in a covenant relationship dishonor his covenant partner? Why would you no longer want to meet with your covenant partner, and why would you think of robbing him?

We may learn a lesson from Jesus in regards to covenant relationship. He has traveled to Jerusalem with His parents to observe the Passover. Rather than setting out with them on the return journey after the festival, at the tender age of twelve He is found in the temple with the teachers of the Law. *"Son, why have you treated us like this?"* asks His worried mother (Luke. 2:48). *"Why were you searching for me? Didn't you know I had to be in my Father's house?"*

comes the confident response (Luke. 2:49). The KJV puts it this way: *"Don't you know I must be about my father's business?"* This is a sentiment that was to be the hallmark of Jesus' life.

The manner of His life was characteristic of a person in covenant relationship with His Father. The complete transparency between Jesus and his Father at once instructs us all as to how we should walk in our relationship both with our soul-mate and with God.

On occasions he told his disciples, *"I tell you the truth, the Son can do nothing by Himself; he can do only what he sees his Father doing, because whatever the Father does the Son also does"* (e.g., John 5:19). *"Father, into your hands I commit my spirit"* (Luke 23:46) were his final words from the cross. He had left the bosom of the Father to come to earth; now he returns to Him. There has to be complete trust between you and the one to whom you would commit your spirit. Jesus longed for fellowship with His Father with whom he had an everlasting covenant.

Family and Worship

The Perpetual Nature of the Covenant
Part V

The topic of covenant is cast in the context of courtship and marriage because of its vital link between the family and worship. As mentioned earlier, a covenant is more than a promise. The former creates a contract that is binding; the latter creates expectation that may or may not be fulfilled.

A relationship, no matter how strong, once entered into solely on a promise can be broken at anytime. A covenant, on the other hand, is permanent and may go beyond the lives of the covenanters. We have, by means of the marriage relationship, illustrated the covenant relationship God has made with us his children.

In building a covenant relationship like marriage, the covenanters must watch their EQ—expectation quotient—to be sure it is not too high. Marriage cannot be viewed as a perpetual honeymoon. It has its challenges. As a covenant relationship, however, it can endure "for better, for worse," "in sickness and in health," and "for richer, for poorer."

What is said of the covenant of marriage can also be said of the covenant relationship God entered into with some of his choice servants in the Bible. Divine covenant relationship was never a perpetual honeymoon. It had its valleys, its trials, and its challenges.

By the time God called Moses (Ex. 3), covenanting had become the chief method by which He dealt with His chosen people, particularly those whom He drafted into special service. Moses, whose call came through the medium of a burning bush, is a good example. Called out of the wilderness by the medium of the burning bush, He responded positively to the divine voice. One day, he stood gazing in astonished fascination at the miracle of the crackling flames of a tree on fire but not being scorched or consumed. Out of the flames thundered a voice: *"Moses, Moses!"* Swiftly came Moses' answer: *"Here I am"* (Ex. 3:4, NIV). *"Take off your sandals, for the place where you are standing is holy ground"* (Ex. 3:5). This is the beginning of a life of "adventure" with God. **"Would becoming a servant of God be always filled with this kind of excitement?"** he may have asked himself.

Initial enchantment with the divine quickly evaporated when God gave Moses his life's assignment: *"I am sending you to Pharaoh to bring my people the Israelites out of Egypt"* (v. 10). **"Oh no. I can't do it,"** Moses protested. **"I have never been eloquent, neither in the past nor since you speak to me. I am slow of speech."** Not merely a speech defect, as many believe, mind you. Rather he was rusty from being in the wilderness for forty years, where the most part communication was with all but sheep. It's like saying, **"I've have had no intellectual stimulation for forty years; how can you expect me to go into courts with Pharaoh?"** But God knew that if anyone could enter the courts of Pharaoh, Moses could. After all, he was a Pharaoh, except that he refused the name in preference of his racial

Part V

identity. *"By faith Moses, when he had grown up, refused to be known as the son of Pharaoh"* (Heb. 11: 24, *NIV*).

God's commission may have coaxed an unwilling "yes" out of Moses, but he was not in a state of mental confusion. Foremost at the back of his mind must have been the way and the reason he left Egypt. It must have been a daunting task knowing that he was asked to go back to the very Egypt he fled forty years earlier for murder. How would he face the Pharaoh whose kin he had killed?

Of course, all this is so typical of marriage relationships. After the glitter of the honeymoon you must now go to work to make the relationship work. When the fascination with the fire racing through the brushes is over, it is time for serious business. It is time to move out of your comfort zone, risky as it is.

Moses manufactured excuses like they were coming off an assembly line. I am insufficient for Pharaoh. I am slow of speech. What if the children of Israel do not believe me? Who do I tell Pharaoh sent me?

In all of this, God knew the only thing that would make Moses comfortable going to Egypt was making a covenant with him. So He gave Moses his covenant word: *"I will be with you"* (Ex. 3: 12, *NIV*). Struggling with the weight of his assignment, but understanding the nature of covenant, *"Moses took his wife and his sons, put them on a donkey and started back to Egypt"* (Ex. 4: 20, *NIV*).

Moses once having made his decision to go to Egypt, his strife ceased. No longer did he question God. He understood the nature of covenant. Once God convinced him that He would be with him, Moses knew he had all one needed to face any foe.

Family and Worship

It was such a covenant that gladdened the sad and fearful hearts of the disciples when the dreaded task of evangelizing the world was committed into their feeble hands. *"Therefore, go and make disciples of all nations, baptizing them in the name of the Father and of the Son and of the Holy Spirit, and teaching them to obey everything I have commanded you. And surely I am with you always, to the very end of the age"* (Matt. 28:19-20, NIV). Why all the way to the "end?" Because no covenant is intended to stop short of the end. If Jesus goes with you, it will be to the end. Little wonder the song writer says, **"When I come to the river at the ending of day, when the last winds of sorrow have blown, there'll be somebody waiting to show me the way, I won't have to cross Jordan alone."**

When persecution had robbed the early church of all its original leaders, all but John, and his life hung by a slender thread, Jesus appeared to him on the barren and desolate Isle of Patmos, out in the middle of the raging Aegean Sea. Showing himself as the covenant-making and covenant-keeping One, He came to him in the midst of his distress and comforted him with these words of inspiration: *"I am the Alpha and the Omega"* (Rev. 1:8). By his presence Jesus was saying, **"My covenant with you is good for all time and for all places, whether you are in Patmos or Palestine."** Might this be Paul's discovery that gave rise to his timeless statement that has for so long supported us when the tides of life seemed to be overwhelming? *" Who shall separate us from the love of Christ? Shall trouble or hardship or persecution or famine or nakedness or danger or sword... I am convinced that neither death nor life... will be able to separate us from the love of God that is in Christ Jesus our Lord"* (Rom. 8:35-38, NIV).

Part V

Hardly does a journey consist of all level ground with garden-like scenery or straight velvet paved roads. What is true of the physical is also true of the spiritual. No matter life's terrain, covenant, be it with man or with God, is binding and abiding. Sometimes we may be up and some times we may be down, but nothing invalidates the covenant. As a matter of fact, when we are up, the covenant protects us from what we may consider doing to our covenant partner; and when we are down, it protects us from what our partner may consider doing to us.

You and I know all too well that some people cheer you on when things are good, but are not to be found when they are bad. The man who came to be known to us as the prodigal son (Luke 15) learned that the hard way. Taking all his inheritance and belongings, he left home and squandered it all with his friends. *"After he had spent everything,* says Luke, *"there was a severe famine in the land..."* (v.14). Once the famine hit, it was every man for himself. All his friends forsook him. In dire need of food, he hired out himself to feed pigs, and *"longed to fill his stomach with the pods that the pigs were eating, but no one gave him anything"* (v. 16).

As has been demonstrated from chapter one, there is a similarity between the covenant we make in marriage and the covenant we make when we accept Christ as Savior. If this is the case, what must we make of divorce? I must hasten to tell you that even though we have divorce in our society, it does not change the intent or the spirit of the divine covenant. Divorce allowed by God in the Old Testament (Deut. 24:1-3; Jer. 3:8) was not an indication of a change in His original intent, but rather that it might be perpetuated. That is, if the marriage relationship is a reflection of the relationship between Christ and His church, (Eph. 5.20) a bad marriage is a bad reflection of the ideal.

Family and Worship

Since one marriage is, however, only a microcosm of the institution of marriage, the breakdown of one does not mean that the institution as a whole has broken down, anymore than a bad church or a bad church leader does not mean that the church is bad or broken down. You see, the covenant is stronger than the individual and the institution larger and more enduring than the individual.

At this point, we might do well to ask: *"how do we perpetuate ourselves in marriage?"* Through reproduction!

So, what is the spiritual implication? How do we perpetuate ourselves spiritually?

No sooner than we have settled in with God and have come to know Him, we should seek to produce spiritual offspring. And they should be legitimate! They should be ours, not by invitro fertilization or by artificial insemination. That is, not by any artificial means. They should be born of the water, the Spirit, and the blood. Note the behavior of the early church or even the disciples. Upon finding Jesus, Andrew went with extraordinary joy and excitement and boldly told his brother Peter, *"I have found the Messiah"* (Jn. 1: 42).

Rarely have I seen newly weds that found out they were going to have their first child and were not filled with excitement. Nor have I seen one who did not call home to share the good news with family and friends. In fact often, anxious to forecast it to the world, they would go out and purchase maternity clothes. It should be no different with sharing the gospel. There can be nothing more exciting than knowing that both God's will and our desires are fulfilled in the marriage.

While there are those in the natural world who delay child bearing, spiritually there is no reason to delay bringing others into the kingdom. Some who delayed and squandered their only chance have entered eternity with the sad refrain on their lips: *"Must I go and empty handed, must I meet my Savior so, not one soul with which to greet Him, must I empty handed go?"* **Do not wait, child of God. Do not wait! Arise, oh child of God, arise!** Bring forth children for Christ, for soon the time of childbearing will be over and empty handed to Jesus you may go. Let us work while it is day, for the night comes when no one can work.

Let me introduce you to another role children play in a marital relationship. It is noticeable that a couple is more likely to stay married rather than divorce because of the strong, intricate ties that children bring to the conjugal relationship. Children embody the investment, love, hope and promise of both parents, and provide them something to live for. So, also, the Christian who gives birth is more tolerant and is less likely to leave the kingdom at the sound of the first wind because of the intricate ties he shares with his converts. The persons he has won to Christ provide the soul-winner something to live for.

A community in which people are marrying and having children can never become extinct. Its streets will always be filled with the sweet voices of youth—its hope of perpetuation! The church that is winning new converts will also buzz with the sweet voices of its young—its hope of the future. Covenant is perpetual in nature, and perpetuation is at its heart.

Covenant Bonding of the Natural and Spiritual

Christ's Return and the Marriage of the Lamb
Part VI

You might recall that the series, "A Call to Covenant Relationship," started with mate selection, meandering through marriage and many aspects of family life, oscillating between the natural and the spiritual implications and applications, with the intent of making the topic clear and practical. An interesting journey it has been indeed! We have, throughout this discourse, used the relationship between God and Israel and other special people he called to fill in the pieces of the divine jigsaw puzzle. As Jack O. and Judith K. Balswick in their book *A Christian Perspective on the Contemporary Home* state, "The relationship between God and the children of Israel has proven to be the most fruitful model for the development of a theology of the family"* (p. 20). That relationship also illustrates God's covenant relationship with the Church.

Covenant Bonding of the Natural and Spiritual

The first words of the covenant God made with Noah are: *"I will establish my covenant with you, and you will enter the ark-you and your sons and your wife and your sons' wives with you"* (Gen. 6:18). Without questioning God, Noah did what he commanded. Not long after, God repeated the promise of the covenant—this time with a change of tense: *"Now I establish my covenant with you and with your descendants after you and with every living creature that was with you "* **(Gen. 9: 9, NIV).**

The next references to covenant are in Genesis 15:18 and 17:1-7, where God promises to bless Abraham and his descendants. The spiritual implication of a covenant can rarely be separated from its natural application. God's covenant relationship with Israel, or chosen individuals, is fraught with symbolic implication of which marriage is one. It is no coincidence then that the marriage of the Lamb is mentioned in the very last book of the Bible (Rev. 19).

Courting couples find ways of surprising each other far beyond our wildest imagination, all the while creatively attempting to show love. In Matthew 25, Jesus tells the parable of the ten virgins. With watchfulness as its major theme, the illustration is all about the fact that Jesus is coming back for his waiting bride, the Church, in the fullness of time. The return of Christ is as a groom to a bride. This means all that has happened from Genesis to Revelation, from Eden to the coming of Christ, is no more than a courtship—divine courtship that is! And the goal of courtship is marriage. The bride must always be ready and waiting, because the bridegroom is coming.

Misunderstanding and serious debate about the rapture of the Church and the coming of Christ have always been a part of Christianity from its earliest beginnings. For example,

Part VI

the Thessalonians were confused as to what would happen to the believers who died before the coming of the Lord. Paul instructed them: *"Brothers, we do not want you to be ignorant about those who fall asleep, or to grieve like the rest of men, who have no hope. We believe that Jesus died and rose again and so we believe that God will bring with Jesus those who have fallen asleep with Him... For the Lord Himself will come down from heaven with a loud command, with the voice of the archangel and with the trumpet call of God, and the dead in Christ shall rise first. After that, we who are still alive and are left will be caught up to meet Him in the air. And so we will be with the Lord forever. Therefore encourage each other with these words"* **(1 Thess. 4:13-17, NIV).**

If these brethren only knew the nature of covenant, they would not have grieved at the passing of any of their loved ones as they did. Indeed, many Christians have died and many more will die, but not even death can change or nullify Christ's covenant. Nothing will change for the living or the dead, according to the above passage, at His coming. Neither in cultures past or present has it been customary for a bridegroom to give the hand of his bride to another. So it is with Christ and his bride, the Church. He might have a heavenly contingent with him; Gabriel might be blowing the trumpet; but none but he Himself is coming for the bride. *"For the Lord 'Himself will come down from heaven"* to escort the bride home. The latter part of the verse says, *"And so shall they be with the Lord forever"* (NIV).

Prior to marriage, the courting couple, madly in love though they might be, must stay apart, sometimes languishing until the set time-the wedding day. Once the wedding takes place, then shall the saying come to pass, *"For this reason a man will leave his father and mother and be united to his wife, and they will become one flesh "* (NIV).

Covenant Bonding of the Natural and Spiritual

Jesus, to re-enforce the importance of the saying, repeated it verbatim, adding, *"Therefore what God has joined together, let not man separate"* (Matt. 19:6, NIV).

Does this not sound like a wedding? *"And so shall they be with the Lord forever"* (I Thess. 4:17). Were I in doubt of his coming, I would most certainly take courage, knowing that not only does the covenant ensure his coming, but that he will Himself come back for me—a part of the espoused bride—and nothing can hinder it!

The Corinthians had questions about the resurrection of deceased believers and the return of Christ. It is this search for answers that gives rise to Paul's elaborate treatment of the nature of the resurrection in I Corinthians 15. *"...We will not all sleep, but we will be changed -in a flash—in the twinkling of an eye, at the last trumpet. For the trumpet will sound, and the dead will be raised imperishable, and we shall be changed"* (1 Cor. 15: 51, NIV). It is probably no less difficult for you and me to understand the mystery of the resurrection than for the people of Corinth during the time of Paul. It is no easier to understand now than it was then. As in so many things concerning the mystery of our salvation, we will not understand the mystery of the resurrection and the second coming until it actually happens to us; so, without over simplifying the matter, let it suffice that the trumpet "will" sound and we "will" be changed! For the rest of the mystery I can wait!

While the past is always clear, as a result of hindsight, the future always appears fuzzy. And yet, the only instructor of the future is the past. Among the books of the Bible, Revelation is one of the most fascinating. Fascinating in ways more than one. The visions of John have been a challenge to many theologians. However, familiarity with other books of the Bible will discover antecedents to these visions and help unlock their meaning. Among the dazzling sights that John saw is a wedding in heaven. Might this be the key to understanding God's intent for his people? Might this be the reason he so often speaks of and to Israel in nuptial language? It is not only the wedding that I find profoundly engaging, but what precedes it. In Revelation 18:20, we see a great rejoicing in heaven by the conquering saints for the ultimate victory over the kingdom of Babylon-a symbolic representation of the kingdom of evil.

The beauty of the scenery begins in chapter 19. "After these things" suggests that another scene is presented. Chapters 17 and 18 deal primarily with the downfall of the Babylonian world system, and chapter 19 with the final defeat of the Antichrist. Of particular interest is the fact that this scene is introduced not by an angel, but by a chorus of loud voices as of a combined choir singing a hallelujah chorus. It is evident that the song was sung in response to what happened in chapter 18:20, the overthrow of Babylon.

It might be of interest to note that the word **"hallelujah,"** from which we derive the English **"praise the Lord,"** occurs here for the first time in the N.T. and appears four times in this chapter alone (verses 1, 3,4,6). The second "hallelujah," like the first, comes from the same chorus of heavenly singers (v. 3). In verse 4 the 24 elders and the 4 living beings respond to the hallelujah chorus sung by the heavenly choir by falling down before the throne of God in worship, saying *"Amen"* and *"Hallelujah."* **"Amen,"** a Hebrew word translated **"truly,"** shows the positive approval of the 24 elders and the 4 living creatures to what God has done and to the way he has done it.

Covenant Bonding of the Natural and Spiritual

The fourth hallelujah comes in verse 6 with even greater intensity: *"Then I heard what sounded like a great multitude, like the roar of rushing waters and like loud peals of thunder, shouting: "Hallelujah!" For our Lord God Almighty reigns"* (NIV). Now both the 24 elders and the 4 living creatures, backed up by the heavenly choir, are giving glory to God because he reigns, meaning that he is on the throne. That is, he has finally brought all other powers under his control, and now he rules.

During the many weddings that I have been privileged to perform, nothing has fascinated me more than when I get to the part that asks, *"Who gives this woman to be married to this man?"* and to watch the give-away father step aside and witness the groom squaring his shoulders and proudly taking the hand of the bride. It is truly a thing of beauty.

The jubilation and celebration (Rev. 19: 1-6) which precede the announcement of the marriage in verse 7 is very typical of weddings. Verse 7 says, *"Let us rejoice and be glad and give Him glory! For the wedding of the Lamb has come, and her bride has made herself ready"* (Rev. 19:7). Commenting on verse 7, (NIV), the writer of the complete Biblical library it says, *"A further and most important vindication of God's people will be the Marriage Supper of the Lamb, and a great wedding banquet fulfilling the parables and the prophecies, and typologies of the relationship of the church to Christ. This is a further reason to rejoice. When this takes place all the universe will know that the church is what the Bible says the church is, the bride of Christ. It will bring great honor and glory to God the Father as a culmination of His great plan of redemption"* (p. 291).

That God gave John this vision of the end-time was a most splendid way of encouraging the fledgling church, but

Part VI

I don't think we are in any way able to properly imagine the full joy of the end-time will bring. When sorrow rocks our bleeding hearts in a world of sin and distress, just the anticipation of this great event inspires joy beyond our wildest imagination. How much more when the day shall come!

One must waste no time in looking closer at the rest of the verse, because it deepens the sense of the relationship, moving so swiftly from calling the church the "bride" to the "wife." It is indeed a special designation. Jesus, by referring to the Church as the "wife," is suggesting that she has already entered into a full, intimate, loving and personal relationship.

We, the saints, have already entered into a loving relationship with the Master albeit the full consummation has not taken place yet. And, if I'm allowed to personalize this idea, if you are not in a close loving and personal relationship with Him now, don't hope for the consummation of the marriage. If this is not enough to stir courage in the heart of the believer, take a look at the latter part of the verse, "And His wife has made herself ready." The fact that John saw the bride ready is a sure sign that the groom is coming. Know for sure that this is a heavenly vision. It is intended to convey the truths of the future to the church.

As the vision develops, the wife is seen in heaven fully clothed in fine linen, clean and white, pure and spotless. A bride dressed in her wedding garment is a sight to behold! Never does a bride look more beautiful than on her wedding day. But if we step back a bit, we might well see something else. We will see a waiting bride, a ready bride, a complete bride, a pure bride awaiting the arrival of the groom. She is a bride who knows that the groom is coming. Waiting is not a problem for her because she knows that the promise of the groom is sure.

In reminding His people of the faithfulness of His covenant to them, God said the following unto them, *"Sing, O barren woman, you who never bore children; burst into song, shout for joy, you who were never in labor, because more are the children of the desolate woman of her who has a husband, " says the Lord. Enlarge the place of your tent, stretch your tent curtain wide, do not hold back; lengthen your cords strength your stakes. For you will spread out to the right hand and to the left, your descendants will dispossess nations and settle in their desolate cities. Do not be afraid, you will not suffer shame. Do not fear disgrace; you will not be humiliated. You will forget the shame of your youth and remember no more the reproach of your widowhood For your maker is your "husband'–the Lord Almighty is His name ... The Lord will call you back as if your were a "wife" deserted ... a "wife" marry young, only to be rejected,"* says your God (Isa. 54.1-6, *NIV*).

How can the intended intimacy be missed in this Isaiah passage? What sure comfort do such promises bring to an espoused woman! I have no doubt that He's coming back again. I've got the engagement ring -the down payment- the arrabon, and I'm waiting, and it won't be in vain. Some would have us believe that our hope is vain. But, if God's dealing with his people in the past is anything to go by, the future is bright! Waiting awhile you may, but coming he is! The covenant with His people cannot be fulfilled in its totality in this life with its imperfections.

Robert H. Mounce noted that "In Biblical times marriage involved two major events, the betrothal and the wedding. These were normally separated by a period of time during which the two individuals were considered husband and wife and as such were under the obligation of faithfulness..." *New International Commentary on the New Testament* (1977, p. 340). This period of separation, however, was only temporary however long it lasted. It is in this vein that God, in reestablishing His covenant with His people, spoke by the prophet Hosea saying, *"In that day, " declared the Lord, "you will call me 'my husband'; you will no longer call me 'my master'. . . . I will betroth you to me forever I will betroth you in righteousness and justice, in love and compassion"* (Hosea 2: 16, 19). God intends more than a casual relationship with His people. That he is in heaven and we are on earth is only a temporary arrangement as in a betrothal. His return is certain. The life of husband and wife cannot be lived effectively from a distance.

Paul, in one of his profound and animated exhortations to the Ephesians, sets forth the conjugal nature of the husband-wife relationship as a microcosm of the relationship between Christ and His church, and shows us how it should be lived. He ends the passage by saying, *"This is a profound mystery but I am talking about Christ and the church "* (Eph. 5: 32, NIV). It is this mystery that is yet to unfold-and will unfold-because our God is a covenant God. Though He delays, as it may seem to us, He will come. The covenant won't let him stay but for a while.

Delay is always difficult for anyone who is waiting. Jesus, knowing this, warns us of the danger in the story of the Ten Virgins (Matt. 25), which instructs us of the need for watchfulness, patience, and adequate resource. It is certain the bridegroom is coming, but the time of his coming is uncertain. Tarry he might, but come he will! Covenant requires it.

Covenant Bonding of the Natural and Spiritual

As told by Matthew, part of the wedding party was surprised by the groom's arrival because they had failed to make provision for the long haul. If you are asking, **"How long, Lord, how long?"** don't despair. Many others of God's people have asked the same question. And, doubtlessly, the ten virgins, too! Yet, no sooner than the ten virgins fell asleep, the echo of the crier's voice was heard splitting the stillness of the midnight, **"Come out to meet him, come out to meet him!"** Only those who were ready and waiting went out to meet him; by the time the others got ready, the door was already shut.

Israel's impatience in waiting for Moses to return from the mount of God where he went to receive the law also had its tragic consequences. Conscripting Aaron to make them a golden calf as an object of worship, soon they engaged in wild exuberance. It was this idolatrous frenzy Moses encountered as he came down from the mountain that sent him into a rage. Stunned by it all, he impetuously shattered on the ground the tablets of stone written with the very finger of God. Worse still, he had about three thousand of the Israelites killed (Exod. 32:28).

Waiting is always difficult. No one can deny that sometimes we too in our despondency are apt to make hasty choices. If you have that tendency, remember you are not playing the stock market in which you may lose your shirt today and win a dozen shirts tomorrow. Waiting for Christ's return is a matter of eternal consequences. History evidences the slowness with which God sometimes moves, from man's point of view, but history has no less proven that when His time is right, He swiftly accomplishes his promises.

One day our long wait for the bridegroom will come to an end. He will come to take his bride away. **"Blessed** *are they which are called unto the marriage supper of the Lamb"* (Rev. 19.9, KJV). This is what John was told to write immediately after his vision of the bride dressed in fine white linen, which is also the appropriate and symbolic attire of the saints. That the blessed ones are **"called"** is of great importance and implication. **Called** is an operative, suggesting not only that they are invited but that they have accepted the invitation.

In antiquity, as here, it was never the bride that went for the groom, but the groom that went for the bride. Mounce says, *"The wedding begins with a procession to the bride's house, which was followed by a return to the house of the groom for the marriage feast. By analogy, the church, espoused to Christ by faith, now awaits the parousia when the heavenly groom will come for his bride and return to heaven for the marriage feast which will last throughout eternity"* **Ibid** (I.C. N.T. p. 340). The imagies of **marriage** and **marriage feast** are not without significance. We may go to a marriage feast corporately, but the marriage is a relationship into which only two people are invited. We can enter into a living personal relationship with the Lord only on an individual basis.

Just as any bride would await her bridegroom with eager anticipation, perhaps even taking an intermittent peep through the window hoping to catch sight of him as rounds the bend to take her away, so the Church should expectantly await the coming of Christ. Jesus' promise is sure: *"I go to prepare a place for you. And if I go and prepare a place for you, I will come again, and receive you unto myself; that where I am, there you may be also"* (John. 14: 2, 3, KJV).

Oh, that we had the divine perspective on things! Caught up to heaven, John the revelator saw the wedding as a

Covenant Bonding of the Natural and Spiritual

transpiring reality. *"Let us rejoice and be glad and give him glory! For the wedding of the Lamb has come, and his bride has made herself ready. Fine linen, bright and clean, was given her to wear,"* the heavenly voice told him (Rev. 19:7, 8). The bride, all ready and waiting in heaven, shows God's perspective on what he has promised. The **"shall bell"** is already done. It just has not caught up to us yet.

It might be that there are those of us who, after two thousand years, have begun to wonder if we have been misinformed. If you happen to be one of them, be encouraged. It is already done. If you could see what John saw and understood what John understood, you would do what he did in acknowledgement of what is prepared for us. According to verse 10, the wonder, the joy, the blessedness and the hope the vision inspired so overwhelmed him that he bowed in worship.

Noticeable in the narrative is the sudden switch from the vision of the marriage supper of the Lamb to an angel standing in the sun (19:17). This sets the stage for the final judgment. In order for the marriage of the Lamb to be completed Satan must be brought under control. The interruption of man's relationship with God between Genesis and Revelation was caused by Satan's interference. So, before the marriage is fully realized Satan must be taken out of the way. In a word, before the new order can be established, the old order must be abolished.

Now that we have come past the judgment of Satan and Babylon, we arrive at chapter 21 where a new and different vision bursts on John's sight: a new heaven and a new earth—what I consider to be preparation for the completion of the marriage. There is nothing that a new bride looks forward to more than a new place of residence. Be assured

Part VI

that Jesus the groom of the church will ensure for us the very best; not a renovated place, but a brand new one.

The New Jerusalem is different from anything we know. It is truly a holy place set apart for the Lamb and his bride. There will be no violation of privacy as in the Garden of Eden. The meeting of God with man will never be interrupted; it will be free from any intruder whose motive is other than pure.

"And I heard a loud voice from the throne saying, "Now the dwelling of God is with men, and He will live with them. They will be His people, and God Himself will be with them and be their God. He will wipe every tear from their eye. There will be no more death or mourning or crying or pain, for the old order of things has pass away" (21:3, 4 NIV). Considering that John was placed on the Isle of Patmos that he might die, what sweet assurance it must have been to hear that voice speaking such words of comfort to him. All at once, the groom is offering all the comfort that is often lavished on a new bride, such as removing all tears. Removing tears from one's eye is a sign of consummate intimacy, yet as sweet as that must have sounded, the best was yet to come: there shall be no more death. This is the ultimate. After all, no one minds crying a little if they'll be free of death. What blessed assurance!

It is interesting how eternity has come full circle. The Bible begins with the words, **"In the beginning God created the heavens and the earth. "** Here at the end we hear the words, **"Behold I make all things new."** In eternity past God was all, and in the future He will be all in all. The first creation would have mystified man had he been there to witness each act. Can you imagine light springing up out of nowhere all of a sudden at the command of the Omnipotent? Little wonder

Covenant Bonding of the Natural and Spiritual

John was beside himself when he saw the New Jerusalem coming down from God out of heaven!

Now that God has completed preparation for the bride—the New Jerusalem—the next thing the angel shows John is a beautiful pure river of water of life coming out of the throne of God and the Lamb and flowing down through the street of gold in the middle of the city. Whatever else this might mean, one thing is clear—even in the New Jerusalem everything and everyone will depend on God for life and sustenance. The picture is reminiscent of Genesis 2: 10. Where there is no water there is no life! If you want to know, there will be real life in the New Jerusalem and there will be no lack.

After showing John the idyllic state in which the saints will exist, the angel told John not to seal up the prophetic book (cf. Dan. 12:4) because the time of its fulfillment is near (Rev. 22: 10). Then, in the home stretch, John hears the stirring words of Jesus, *"And behold, I come soon! My reward is with me, and I will give to everyone according to what he has done"* (22:12, NIV). Then, He gives us His very own signature, *"I am the Alpha and the Omega, the first and the last, the beginning and the end* (22:13). He wanted John to have no misgivings about who was speaking to him. Nor does he want us to have any!

Despite the innumerable prophecies throughout the Old Testament concerning the Messiah's first coming, when He arrived many of his people did not believe He was the promised One. The skepticism of the world allowed Him to sneak in incognito. If the same thing were to happen at His return, the consequences would be all together different. Then He came as redeemer, but this time He will come as judge.

Part VI

I am not able to tell you the time of the Savior's return, but this I can say without equivocation in the words of the song writer, "The King is Coming!."

The market place is empty, no more traffic in the street,
all the builders tools are silent, no more time to harvest wheat.
Busy housewives cease their labor, in the courtroom no debate;
work on earth has been suspended, as the king comes through the gate.

All the railroad cars are empty, as they rattle down the tracks;
in the newsroom no one watches, as machines type pointless facts.
All the planes veer off the runway, no one sits at the control;
for the King of all the ages, comes to claim eternal souls.

Happy faces line the hallways, those whose lives have been redeemed.
Broken homes that He has mended, those from prison He has freed.
Little children and the aged, hand in hand stand all aglow,
who were crippled, broken, ruined, clad in garments white as snow.

I can hear the chariots rumble, I can see the marching throng,
the flurry of God's trumpets spell the end of sin and wrong.
Regal robes are now unfolding, Heaven's grandstands all in place;
heaven's choir is now assembled, as they sing, "amazing grace."

The king is coming, the king is coming; I can hear the trumpets sounding
and, now His face I see. Oh the king is coming;
the king is coming; praise God He's coming for me.

If that does not do it for you, then try this one:

"It Is Finished the Battle Is Over."

There's a line that's been drawn through the ages
on that line, stands an old rugged cross.
On that cross the battle is raging for the gain of man's soul that was lost.
But in my heart the battle was still raging,
I did not know that the battle had been won,
And there stands God's Son in the battle,
and then through the darkness he cried:

Covenant Bonding of the Natural and Spiritual

it is finished, the battle is over; it is finished,
there'll be no more war; it is finished the
end of the conflict, it is finished, and Jesus is Lord!
The end!

Other Books by
George Peart:

Basusu
Wisdom From the Well
Can't See Out of Your Eye

To Order Call:
1-800-553-8506
or visit us on the web at:
www.pathwaybookstore.com

George Peart is also available for conferences.
For Booking Information Call:
905-793-2213
905-867-1512
954-987-7185
or
email:bishop@ontario.org